THEATRE
IN HIGH SCHOOL:
Planning, Teaching,
Directing

PRENTICE-HALL SERIES IN
THEATRE AND DRAMA

Oscar G. Brockett
Consulting Editor

Robert Benedetti, THE ACTOR AT WORK

Charlotte Kay Motter, THEATRE IN HIGH SCHOOL:
PLANNING, TEACHING, DIRECTING

PRENTICE-HALL INTERNATIONAL, INC., *London*
PRENTICE-HALL OF AUSTRALIA, PTY. LTD., *Sydney*
PRENTICE-HALL OF CANADA, LTD., *Toronto*
PRENTICE-HALL OF INDIA PRIVATE LIMITED, *New Delhi*
PRENTICE-HALL OF JAPAN, INC., *Tokyo*

THEATRE IN HIGH SCHOOL:
Planning, Teaching, Directing

CHARLOTTE KAY MOTTER

Canoga Park High School
Los Angeles, California

PRENTICE-HALL INC., Englewood Cliffs, New Jersey

13-913012-8

Library of Congress Catalog Card Number: 71–125559

Printed in the United States of America

Current printing (last number):

10 9 8 7 6 5 4 3 2 1

To my mother, Opal Eduard Motter,
actress, director, and teacher,
who did not teach me everything I know—
but almost everything!

Preface

There are few sources of information about the specific problems of high school drama, except rare articles in professional periodicals like *The Educational Theatre Journal, The Bulletin of Secondary School Principals, The English Journal,* and *Dramatics.* These articles indicate so wide a variety of programs and philosophies of educational theatre that they sometimes contribute more to the confusion than to the enlightenment of the neophyte. Although some of these materials are good, they are scattered and fragmentary because the high school teacher-director has been too busy doing his job to write about how and why and what he does.

Simply stated, this book is my attempt to answer this question: What have I discovered about high school drama by trial and error that someone might have told me before I started to teach drama in high school?

The purpose of this book is to provide a single source of reference for the prospective or beginning high school teacher-director, and to offer more nearly complete information on the multiple problems confronting him on the job.

Much of this material was developed and continually revised during the twelve years that I taught a course called "Drama in the Secondary School" at the University of California, Los Angeles in addition to my job as teacher-director of drama at Canoga Park High School. I have adapted and expanded the material to explore three major aspects of high school drama: first, the present position of drama and the teacher-director in the high schools; second, the relationship of high school drama to the whole curriculum, to the school administration and faculty, and to the community; third, the teaching of drama classes and producing of plays in the high school.

To the experienced high school teacher-director the attempt to cover all of these aspects of high school drama in a single volume will seem somewhat akin to engraving the Gettysburg Address on the head of a pin. It is! But this book does not primarily address itself to experienced instructors, although some of them who feel that there are gaps in their training may find it useful. It is designed to be a practical guide for the beginning teacher-director. It is hoped that it will not only provide him with guideposts along the route, but also occasional refreshment and encouragement which may give him the strength to continue his journey in this most exciting and rewarding teaching field, high school drama!

The philosophy of education and of theatre which underlies, indeed dominates, my career in educational theatre will undoubtedly be apparent throughout this text. The absence of a special chapter on "Philosophy of High School Drama" is not an attempt to deny the existence of a point of view. Rather, it is a recognition that my philosophy pervades every chapter and will therefore be obvious to the reader without a specific statement thereof.

I wish to express my sincere thanks to my students, both high school and university, who have always demanded a quality performance from me, as I have from them. Al Carrillo, formerly head of the Art Department at Canoga Park High School and teacher of Stage Design from 1953 through 1968, is responsible for all of the stage sets which have been used to illustrate this text. I wish to express my appreciation for his designs as well as for his example as teacher and artist. I want to acknowledge my debt and offer my thanks to my drama colleague at Canoga Park High School, Jacqueline A. Melvin, whose critical reading of the manuscript, many useful suggestions, and moral support have been of inestimable value to me in completing this book.

Charlotte Kay Motter
North Hollywood, California

Contents

THEATRE
IN HIGH SCHOOL:
Planning, Teaching,
Directing

ORIENTATION
TO DRAMA IN
THE HIGH SCHOOL

PART **I**

CHAPTER 1

Why Drama in the High School Curriculum?

Any high school, whether its orientation be traditional, progressive, or comprehensive, which has established the three R's in the curriculum ought next to include courses in the theatre arts. The school that either omits drama from the curriculum or places it on the frills list as an extracurricular or cocurricular activity fails to meet its responsibility to its students and to society.

The theatre arts—motion pictures, television, and theatre—are a primary source of information for the mid-twentieth century American. It has been estimated that one third of the nation is in the audience of the theatre arts every evening. Ninety million people watch television; six million see a motion picture; seventy-five thousand attend the theatre. If the high school is to prepare its students to live in American society, it must offer them the opportunity to acquire a basic education in the theatre arts.

The prospective teacher of drama may have to create his position in the high school by persuading the administration of the need and value of the theatre arts in the secondary school. The drama teacher must be able to explain, justify, and promote theatre in the high school program. He must know how to teach the discipline of the theatre and how to explain the importance of theatre in its social context.

It is not presumptuous of the beginning teacher to assume that he is an authority in theatre arts in relationship to others within his school. As such he may be confident of his own ability to initiate a program of high school drama classes and productions. In so doing, the drama teacher should be aware of his responsibility to establish a program that has value both as education and theatre.

The information in this chapter is designed to help the beginning teacher explain drama to an administration so that theatre arts will be included in the curriculum. It will help the teacher assume a confident attitude in his discussions with administrators.

Student Needs Met by Drama

Like all subjects offered in the school, drama can claim a legitimate place in the curriculum only if it meets the needs of the students. A well-planned and well-taught secondary school drama program can satisfy the students' need to:

> Obtain skill in the use of oral language;
> Develop a well-adjusted personality;
> Learn to cooperate with others;
> Attain approval;
> Develop a capacity for intellectual recreation;
> Develop an appreciation of aesthetic and cultural concepts.

Although many of these needs may be met by other disciplines, some are so specific that they can be obtained only through a drama program. Although the details of classroom and rehearsal methods that satisfy these needs will be the subjects of later chapters, some explanation seems appropriate here.

Skill in the use of oral language is gained through exercises in pronunciation and enunciation, voice development, interpretative reading, and acting. These oral skills are crystallized in the performance of plays.

The most elusive goal in the educational objectives of the drama program is personality development. For good or ill, every experience which a student has makes some impression upon him and affects the kind of individual he eventually becomes. One of the important and desirable traits of personality which drama seeks to develop in a student is his understanding of himself and of others. In his study of the basic psychological factors that motivate the characters in the plays with which he works, he will gain a better understanding of the people he knows. Because play production makes constructive use of a wide variety of talents, it offers every kind of student some challenge at which he can succeed. Each may therefore grow in his own self-esteem which is probably the most universal need of the adolescent. Self-confidence is the result of achievement alone. In finding his niche in high school drama, the student begins to realize the value of his individual traits and the invaluable contribution which he can make to the whole group. A student whose ethnic or religious background sets him apart from the majority of his classmates may be called upon to act as a technical expert when a play requires the enactment of a special ritual or custom associated with his group. Often, for the first time, he begins to see his differences as an asset and develops confidence in being himself. Certainly, an understanding of himself and of others contributes to the development of his personality.

In producing a play, the student learns through practical experience the importance of cooperating with a large group of individuals, each of whom has an assignment integral to the whole production. He observes and works with faculty members as well as other students, each responsible for one of the many facets of the production—directing, acting, stage managing, setting, furnishing, lighting, costuming, publicizing, printing, financing, and selling. This activity emphasizes the interrelation of the parts and the indispensability of each to the whole, and illustrates the importance of obeying the established chain of command vital to any successful cooperative endeavor. He learns that, though everyone is equally important, all are not equal in abilities and responsibilities. He learns that democratic cooperation depends upon an organized plan, a division of responsibilities, and a respect for authority, not upon every individual going his own way with all Chiefs and no Indians.

The theatrical activities of the school provide a means of satisfying the student's need for the approval of his peers. In most schools, students win this approval through athletics, student government, or superior scholarship. But other students should be given the chance to achieve this recognition through drama activities. Perhaps this approbation that the performer receives from the audience is one of the reasons that drama, in some form, is as old as mankind.

By studying theatre and participating in school plays, a student acquires a capacity for intellectual recreation. The modern high school is generously equipped and staffed to provide all forms of physical and manual recreation with gyms, fields, shops, kitchens, and kilns, but the facilities for intellectual recreation seem to be in shockingly short supply. Given the opportunity, the student discovers the excitement of intellectual recreation in making an audience understand and believe the character he is portraying. He finds further stimulation reading and analyzing plays for their plot, structure, theme, characterizations, and emotional content, as well as their literary values. Is not the primary purpose of the school the training of the minds of its students?

Finally, if the school is not actually obliged by its commitment to prepare the student for living to develop in him an understanding and an appreciation of cultural and aesthetic concepts, it should at least encourage this kind of learning. Cultural concepts grow through reading and producing plays wherein the student may discover the beauty of life, the lessons of history, and the problems of society. This is stimulating content for both the instructor and the student of high school drama.

An introduction to an appreciation of aesthetics is another result of study of the theatre arts. The student learns the techniques of establishing a mood that will evoke the desired emotional response from the audience as the arts of light, color, language, interpretation, composition, music, movement, and rhythm are synthesized in a dramatic production. The student learns to enjoy the effectiveness of language which is well-handled in the dialogue of good plays. Through the study of theme and character in dramatic literature he begins to discern that which is universal and timeless in human ideas and experiences.

The high school that offers a program in which theatre is taught as an art can give its students the opportunity to relate to society. The student begins to be connected not merely to his school, community, and nation, but more important to feel himself a part of civilization. This development within the student of a sense of belonging to the whole of mankind is sufficient reason for the inclusion of the theatre arts in the high school.

Effect of Drama Program

In addition to meeting the immediate needs of the high school students, the drama program can develop higher standards of public taste in theatre, improved community relations, guidance of students, and increased respect for the program from other faculty members. Students exposed to a quality high school drama program will eventually demand higher artistic and cultural achievements in living theatre, motion pictures, and television.

A well-designed drama program can be a real asset to the school in its relationships with the community. Parents find that attending a high school play is a pleasure rather than a duty, and other adults become regular members of the audience when the high school offers fare that stimulates rather than insults their intelligence.

Although few high school drama students pursue careers in the theatre (and the high school theatre training is not designed to be primarily prevocational training), they are often helped by their experience in the theatre to find themselves and to develop self-respect and a sense of direction. Drama provides the student with an opportunity to explore ideas and activities and to evaluate his interests, abilities, and limitations. Tomorrow's electricians, commercial artsts, teachers, carpenters, writers, salesmen, and politicians, and theatre artists may be guided to these careers through high school play production activities.

Of great importance to the teacher-director is the changed attitude and genuine support that will come from administration and faculty when they are introduced to a drama program which they can respect academically. Because they are serious educators, they soon tire of defending a frivolous drama program which they can justify only by saying, "The kids do enjoy it, and it is a good way to raise money for the Senior Class!"

Making a Reality of the Dream

The beginning drama teacher who wishes to establish a meaningful program should lay the foundation in his initial interview with the administration. Principals, like everyone else, tend to respect the individual who respects himself. The drama teacher should, therefore, show his self-respect by offering the principal a program that will meet the students' needs, broaden their cultural, aesthetic, and intellectual horizons, and earn the respect of the community.

Once this philosophy is understood and agreed upon, the drama teacher must prove its validity by creating a strong, systematic program which is integrated with the entire school curriculum. He must demonstrate his intetrest in students, especially the so-called problem students, by constructive work with them. The drama teacher who wishes to succeed must offer cooperation and leadership in many nontheatrical activities, such as graduation exercises, teachers' organizations, athletic events, class sponsorship, social activities, P.T.A. programs, and counseling and guidance services. The drama teacher has many special skills which will be useful and appreciated in all of these other areas.

Above all, the teacher must not lose sight of his ideals. He must teach theatre in the high school for the great cultural and intellectual force which it is in civilization, not use drama as an expedient to get the adolescent exhibitionists out of someone else's hair! He may accomplish this by emphasis upon dramatic literature, theatre history, and analysis of living theatre, all of which show theatre to be an academic discipline and an art form.

Finally, the teacher-director in a high school must produce plays of good quality which are so selected as to be worth doing as an artistic director, worth playing as an actor, and worth witnessing as an auditor.

CHAPTER 2

Qualifications
of the Drama
Teacher

In view of the number of high school teachers assigned to direct plays who have no specific theatrical training, a cynic might say that there are no qualifications for a drama teacher, or at best that the only qualification is a willingness to accept the assignment when it is offered. This discussion therefore will deal with the desirable, or perhaps the ideal, qualifications of the high school drama teacher. There is much to encourage the hope that in the near future the director of the school plays, like the director of the school orchestra, will be recognized as a specialist who must have both talent and training in his field. An increasing number of colleges and universities are offering specific courses concerned with teaching and directing theatre in high schools. Led by California, there is a trend toward recognition of drama as an academic major for teaching certification. School administrators, alerted by the nationwide cultural explosion and guided by the 1962 position paper, "The Arts in the Comprehensive Secondary School" of the National Association of Secondary School Principals,[1] are beginning to seek trained specialists in the theatre arts for positions in their schools. Until all schools have trained teacher-directors of drama, however, each teacher must examine his own qualifications and attempt to correct any deficiencies he may discover.

The teacher assigned to drama in the high school has an ethical responsibility to acquire knowledge that fully qualifies him to do the job well. If he is a trained educator he must study and master the art of

[1] Quotations from this paper appear in Chapter 3.

the theatre. If he is a trained director, he must study and master the techniques of teaching. The high school is entitled to have a teacher-director of drama who is equally proficient in both aspects of his dualistic assignment.

Perhaps more knowledge and initiative is demanded of the drama instructor than of any other high school teacher, because he is an educational pioneer in teaching drama. By his performance on the job he must continually prove the value of his program to students, administrators, and parents. Because he will usually work with inadequate textbooks, he must apply great resourcefulness to finding materials for classroom use. Unlike other teachers in the school, he will work largely without supervision, expert advice, or a preplanned course of study. In other words, he is on his own, and the quality of his teaching will depend upon the depth of his knowledge, background, and experience in the theatre arts. The high school drama teacher is unique among teachers in that he is under constant pressure to produce plays that are successful financially as well as artistically. The product of his teaching is displayed publicly, so that he cannot long deceive anyone about its quality!

Tangible Qualifications

One who expects to become a capable teacher-director of high school drama must meet the minimum educational requirements, which in most states include a bachelor's degree and practice teaching. So that his training includes both theatre and education, he should have a major in drama and a minor in education. His college courses should include extensive study of theatre history and dramatic literature and both theoretical and practical work in acting, directing, and all phases of technical theatre. In brief, his background must be so thorough as to equip him to produce quality theatre in a situation in which no other person has any theatre training. Since the drama activities in nearly all schools remain under the jurisdiction of the English department, the drama teacher will probably find it necessary to obtain either an additional major or minor in English in order to qualify for a teaching job. The prospective director's study in education should include educational philosophy and psychology and, most of all, practice teaching under the guidance of a master teacher of drama. Because no teacher's education is ever completed, most high school teachers will acquire a master's degree or its equivalent within a few years. This graduate study will, of course, be most valuable to the drama teacher (and therefore to his students), if it is concentrated upon advanced work in theatre. Whatever experience he can obtain in professional, community, or summer theatre will also be of inestimable value to the high school director.

Because of the varied and strenuous demands inherent in the teacher-director's job, certain personal qualifications may be essential. He must either have or develop a reasonably pleasant personality, for his job requires that he work with more faculty members and more members of the community than most classroom teachers are required to do. The drama program is interwoven with the school's public relations. The long after-school hours that must be spent in rehearsals and the construction of scenery demand at least average physical health of the director. Even more important, he must have superior mental health, if he is to deal successfully and tactfully with the variety of persons with whom he works and to withstand the nervous tension that always accompanies the responsibility for public performances. When that inevitable moment arrives, during the production process, when all of the elements of the show seem to be in a hopeless tangle, it is vital that the director be able to summon his sense of humor instead of pushing the panic button. He must always take his work seriously, but never take himself too seriously.

Intangible Qualifications

Beyond the qualifications that have been listed are those neither required in the teacher-training curriculum nor enumerated on the teaching certificates—those intangible qualities of spirit and purpose that make a good teacher.

First among these is a sense of mission. In order to do justice to his job, the drama teacher must believe in the importance of his work. He must believe that teaching is a work worth devoting his life to and that theatre is a vital subject in general education.

He must possess an idealism which can never degenerate into cynicism. The idealist is one who believes that ultimately there is more good than evil, more truth than deceit in mankind. When the idealist lacks either the strength or the courage or the patience to prove this philosophy of faith, he becomes a cynic and disqualifies himself to be a teacher. The high school director, by definition of his role as teacher and as artist, must retain his idealism, for without it neither education nor art has any reason for being.

The drama teacher also needs initiative that continually renews itself, and does not merely supply that first spurt of energy accompanying every new undertaking.

In order to find the means of adequately staging plays that have educational value, the director will need to employ creative imagination. He cannnot approach his production problems as he would in a fully equipped professional theatre. Rather, he must find new and often simplified techniques of production, which will allow him to offer to the high school plays of good quality so produced as to transmit faithfully the playwright's intention.

To a greater degree than most other theatrical directors, the high school director must have drive. He must not only maintain his own enthusiasm and forward thrust during the rehearsal period, but must also supply this drive for the students and faculty with whom he works. It is relatively easy to capture the interest and mobilize the energy of everyone concerned during the early stages of production when the challenge of a new experience is present and also during the final days of preparation when the pressure of time is apparent. A unified artistic production, however, cannot be thrown together the last day in the afternoon, so the director must see to it that both enthusiasm and diligent work are sustained throughout the rehearsal period. The director's drive is essential during the doldrums of mid-production.

One of the oldest clichés in education is that the teacher must love kids. To the beginning teacher, this idea can suggest all kinds of frightening images of himself being surrounded by mobs of wild teenagers, even during his after-school hours, and supposedly enjoying himself. What the truism really means is that one who is well-suited for the teaching profession must love people. The teacher should have an interest in society and in the individuals who compose it. He must care what happens to people singly and collectively. Because it is prerequisite both to becoming a true theatrical artist and to becoming a good teacher, the high school director must have a social conscience.

In order to execute the diverse responsibilities of his job, the teacher-director must be thoroughly honest with himself in recognizing his abilities and his limitations. He must know, among the multiple trades of the theatre, of which he is a master and of which he is merely a Jack. If, for example, he is inept with a paintbrush or clumsy with a needle, he can always find expert assistance once he admits his need for help. One may find anything from a seamstress to a fencing master on most high school faculties. On the other hand, the director who knows how to construct a stage flat should not allow the shop teacher, who may glue every joint, to interfere with the proper techniques of stage carpentry. The director who can evaluate his own skills will know when to seek help and thereby will be enabled to do the best possible job.

Most important of all, the drama teacher should be a practical craftsman rather than a temperamental artist. Those directors who dress eccentrically and react hysterically when any problem arises, operate with the delusion that the more difficult they are the more artistic they will become. The true artist is seldom unreasonable or temperamental. Temperament is the camouflage that the inadequate director uses when his knowledge is not sufficient to solve his production problem. A competent teacher-director will not find it necessary to resort to childish temper tantrums when things go awry. Instead he will quietly analyze the problem and begin working on a solution.

Inspirational Teaching

Because his background in the arts and humanities must include a concern for individuals, and because the nature of his job necessitates an intimate knowledge of his students, the drama teacher has a unique opportunity to offer his students a rare educational experience—inspirational teaching.

The most admirable qualities of every individual are usually the result of someone else's faith in him—often an inspiring teacher. There is certainly no simple formula—two measures of courage, one of understanding, and one of hope—that will produce an inspiring teacher, but some characteristics seem to be common to such teachers.

It should be the goal of a teacher to help each student believe in himself. The teacher must somehow find time to know each student as an individual and to discover his special abilities. Once he understands a student, the teacher is able to offer him genuine guidance and to demand the best that he is capable of achieving. One of the greatest services a teacher can perform is to insist that each student contribute to the class the highest quality of work of which he is capable. If the teacher can transmit his belief in each student's ability, he will be an inspiring teacher.

Albert Einstein told us that mankind is here for the sake of others. The teacher-director can be inspiring when he approaches his job with this attitude. He should be directing in order to meet the needs of others rather than to satisfy his own ego. The combination of the attractive personality with which the theatre person is usually endowed and the tendency of adolescents toward hero worship often gives the drama teacher a great deal of influence among his students. He should frequently remind himself that personal magnetism is an asset only when it is used wisely for the benefit of his students.

What is a Teacher?

A teacher plays so many different roles that it is difficult to define his job. What is a teacher? He is what the specific situation and particular moment demand that he be in order to solve the immediate and long range problems of his students. In attempting to play many roles, the teacher may become utterly confused. Perhaps it is easier to list some of the things which a teacher is not so that he may be cautious when he finds himself in the wrong role.

A teacher is not another student. Especially when he begins to teach, he may be more nearly the age of his students than the age of his faculty colleagues. It is his duty to develop a mature outlook and to identify himself with the faculty rather than with the students.

A teacher is not a parent to his students. Although he will meet many students who seem to lack (either actually or practically) a mother or father, the teacher must remember that he has neither the obligation nor the right to assume the role of a parent.

A teacher is not a missionary. He may often feel that the need is such that he should convert the world, but his job is not to save souls or to convince students of the righteousness of his own beliefs. His job is to train the minds of his students. If he is really good at his job of teaching, his students may tend to think of him as perfect, and idolize him. The teacher, like the actor, must beware of believing his own press agents. He is neither perfect nor infallible, and he must remind himself that it is only his student's view of him, through rose colored glasses, which occasionally makes him seem to be so.

A teacher is not a policeman nor a warden. Order and discipline are prerequisite to any constructive work in the classroom, but the teacher who must continually stand guard over his classes has failed to understand the nature of his job. The skill of his teaching rather than the power of his position should maintain discipline in the classroom. Those few students who refuse to respond to skillful teaching should be referred to those persons in the school who are hired to be wardens and policemen.

A teacher is not a judge. Although he must evaluate each student in his own class, he must avoid passing sentence upon any student. No teacher has the right to pass judgment upon a student that will classify him as either worthy or unworthy.

A teacher is not a psychologist nor a psychiatrist. The classroom should never be turned into a pseudo-psychiatric clinic even by the teacher with some training in psychology. This temptation is perhaps greater for the drama teacher than for many others because the nature of his work allows him to observe his students closely and to know them well. It is the job of the classroom teacher to help the normal student adjust to life and to refer the neurotic or psychotic student to a qualified expert.

What, then, is a teacher? In our society he is, must be, all of these things—student, parent, missionary, policeman, judge, and psychologist—blended in equal proportions and perfect balance so that no single element is ever dominant.

Finally the teacher-director must qualify as a skilled artist and craftsman in the theatre and as an unselfish leader in society. He must understand the the importance of his job and believe in his own ability to do that job.

CHAPTER 3

The Status of Drama
in High Schools

Drama in the high schools has not been considered important enough to become the subject of educational research. Although every high school engages in some play production activities, to what extent these are extracurricular and to what extent an outgrowth of drama classes is unknown. Necessarily therefore, the discussion in this chapter is based upon personal observation, experience, and opinion.

Curricular Status of Drama

The place of drama in the school curriculum is largely a reflection of society's attitudes toward the theatre arts. Our Puritan heritage has been evident in the attitude that theatre, if given encouragement by the schools, may lead our children to lives of sin. It is all right for them to act in the Christmas pageant or even the senior play, but we wouldn't want our daughters to become actresses. The suspicion that theatre is somehow immoral may be one reason why schools have been reluctant to offer courses in drama. Why this fear of developing professionals has not extended to the teaching of poetry, music, and painting in the schools is a mystery. In spite of the Puritan background, or perhaps in rebellion against it, drama classes entered the high school curriculum in increasing numbers during the thirties, forties, and early fifties.

Probably the fund-raising potentials of the Junior and Senior play aroused an interest in theatre on the part of school administrators. As schools expanded from purely academic institutions into centers for the social, physical, and recreational activities of teenagers, drama classes were added to the curriculum as elective courses.

It might be said that in encouraging the growth of drama classes in the high schools, curriculum developers were doing the right thing for the wrong reasons. Drama classes were recommended for personality development and as therapy for socially maladjusted students. Dramatic activities provided recreation for students' leisure time.

By 1950 drama was well-established as an elective course in most high schools. It was usually associated with the English department. Russia's Sputnik and Harvard's Conant threw the high schools into a panic in the late fifties. Drama, along with the other arts and humanities, suffered while curricula requirements increased in mathematics and science. Partly because it was soon discovered that all students cannot become scientists and partly because teachers of the arts and humanities were roused to action, the overemphasis on science and math was short-lived in the high school curriculum. For drama educators, this era proved to be a blessing because it forced them to reevaluate their objectives and redefine their place in education. Courses in drama are now gaining a firm place in the high school curriculum because they are being better defined, constructed, and understood.

Beginning with the 1960 Golden Anniversary White House Conferences on Children and Youth, a number of significant events have contributed to improvement of the status of the arts, including the theatre arts, in public education. Among the recommendations of the White House conference were the following:

> That schools provide youth with opportunities for participation in creative dramatics, creative writing, and dramatic productions, under qualified leadership, to develop their talents and give them a basic understanding and critical appreciation of the theatre arts;
>
> That young people be given the opportunity to participate in dramatic productions, under the direction of qualified leaders, in order to acquire the emotional and intellectual disciplines inherent in the theatre arts;
>
> That the curriculum include a program of motion picture and drama appreciation;
>
> That all schools make special provisions for the education of the gifted, talented, and creative student;
>
> That communities provide more theatre facilities.

In September of 1962, the newly created National Council of the Arts in Education, made up of representatives of professional associations of artists and educators in the arts, held its first annual National Conference on the Arts in Education. The recommendations, by this conference, that a comprehensive study of the arts in American life be undertaken and that specialists in art, music, dance, and theatre arts be added to the staff of the Office of Education have been partially implemented.

President Kennedy's appointment of August Heckscher as Special Consultant on the Arts, in the spring of 1962, marked the beginning of the federal government's active concern with and support of the arts. "The Arts and the National Government" was submitted by Mr. Heckscher to the President in May 1963. It reported on the conditions and the needs of the arts in America and contained much information upon which subsequent action by the President and Congress has been based. Commenting on the effect of the National Defense Education Act, Heckscher recommended

> that further consideration be given to increasing the share of the federal government's support to education which is concerned with the arts and the humanities. This should include the same type of across-the-board assistance now given to modern languages, mathematics, and sciences; for example, facilities and equipment, teacher training, teaching techniques and materials, scholarship and fellowship programs. The predominant emphasis given to science and engineering implies a distortion of resources and values. . . .[1]

In immediate response to Heckscher's report, the President's Advisory Council on the Arts was established on June 12, 1963.

Later, the establishment by Congress of the National Arts Council and the enactment of an Arts and Humanities Act and the Elementary and Secondary Education Act gave impetus to the improvement and expansion of the arts in education, through recognition of their values as well as with financial support.

Paralleling the federal government's recognition of the value of the arts to society, their value in education was proclaimed in September 1962 by the National Association of Secondary School Principals' Bulletin in the publication of the NASSP's curriculum position paper, "The Arts in the Comprehensive Secondary School." This paper states:

> The Association firmly believes that the subjects taught and the experiences provided for all children in the area of the arts as defined here are essential to the general education of *all* secondary school youth. The arts in this paper are basically conceived to include the fields of music, visual arts, theatre arts, and some aspects of home economics and industrial arts. . . .
>
> The arts are subject disciplines which emphasize the use of the intellect as well as the development of sensitivity, creativity, and the capacity to make reasoned, aesthetic decisions. . . . The arts give direction to man's patterns of living from the setting of his table to the expression of his most cherished aspirations. The arts constitute a vast communication system which complements man's cognitive word sytsem.

[1] Document No. 28, 88th Cong., 1st sess., 1963.

Although attitudes toward drama in the high school curriculum have been changed by these events, development of the full potential of drama in the schools is still inhibited by high school graduation and college entrance requirements. Drama remains an elective course and students, especially those preparing for college, have little time for electives. In many high schools, drama may be substituted for one of the required classes in English or speech. Building a program in drama, therefore, depends upon creating sufficient interest among students that they will elect advanced courses in the theatre arts, and sufficient interest among administrators that they will schedule these classes.

Improving the Status of Drama

The responsibility for the development of a drama curriculum still lies with the individual teacher. He still labors under the handicap of teaching a subject which many believe requires no training. This belief manifests itself in the persistence of the senior play. As a first step toward establishing respect for the art of theatre, drama teachers should refuse to direct a senior play or any other production which permits students without training to perform. There is little doubt, however, that in theatre, as in music and sports, the outstanding performers have both talent and training. It is also true that very good performances can be delivered by people with relatively little talent, if they have been well trained. If quality performance is the goal of the high school drama teacher, he must insist upon casting his shows with trained student actors. Those directors who claim to do as good a production with untrained students as with trained ones should examine the quality of the training that they give and perhaps reevaluate themselves as teachers.

The actions of the federal government and of the NASSP, cited earlier, indicate that the climate is ideal for the expansion and improvement of secondary school theatre. At long last, there is official recognition of the importance of the arts to the strength of our society. With the support of this recognition from political and educational leaders, the teacher-director should be able to overthrow the tradition of the senior play and develop a program based upon these basic principles:

The purpose of theatre in a school is to educate both the participants and the audience.

The drama classes and the theatrical productions of a high school are part of its curricular educational function, not of its supplemental recreational program.

Theatre education in a high school is primarily general education in the arts and humanities designed to enhance the cultural and aesthetic background of all of the students.

The art of the theatre is a complex discipline with a sequential development and must be taught as such.

Theatrical productions are the product of the sequential discipline of theatre and must evolve from training.

The goal of theatre education is not information but insight; not knowledge but understanding.

The most important lessons of human existence can only be absorbed through empathy; empathy is the wordless, universal language of the theatre.

A drama program based on these principles will gain the respect, support, and interest of faculty and students alike. It will be characterized by classes that strongly emphasize background study of dramatic literature and theatre history as well as acting techniques and technical skills in theatre. The courses offered should be so arranged that mastery of one course is required before a student progresses to the next. Training must be prerequisite to appearing in a school play just as it is in the school orchestra.

Obviously, students with training will produce a better show than the untrained, and in addition, the teacher-director who insists upon training students will be in a stronger position. He will soon find himself teaching all drama classes rather than teaching English classes all day and devoting his after-school hours to producing plays. He will find the quality of his productions greatly enhanced.

The current educational trends inspire much hope that administrators will soon design curricula in the fine arts and seek experts to teach the courses, as they now do in science, English, mathematics, foreign language, and business. Until that day arrives, the status of drama in the high school will continue to depend upon the talent, philosophy, and tenacity of the individual teacher-director.

RELATIONSHIP OF THE DRAMA DEPARTMENT TO THE SCHOOL AND THE COMMUNITY

PART **II**

CHAPTER 4

Relations with Administrators and Faculty

This chapter might be subtitled: Getting Along with the Bosses. Although the faculty and administration of the high school may not literally boss the drama teacher, their attitude toward him and his program control his success or failure. The drama teacher must frequently remind himself that he is not the only teacher in this high school. Drama is not the only valuable subject offered. The drama teacher is not the principal of the high school. In other words, the teacher-director must always respect the interests and positions of those around him.

Initially, administrators and teachers are apt to regard the drama teacher as a kind of mostly harmless nut who, for reasons they do not understand, is a member of every high school faculty. He bears watching lest he gather around him a group of fanatical show-offs and disrupt the entire school with preparations for a production. Unfortunately, their fears may be based upon experience rather than prejudice. Because the chief qualification for a drama teacher has been a willingness to accept the assignment, many jobs have been occupied by teachers who were overdressed and overeager but undertrained. The beginning teacher, therefore, is wise to assume that his colleagues are not prejudiced against him and his subject but wary of both. The drama teacher may have to expend considerable time and energy in educating administrators and faculty members to the values of drama in the school.

If drama is to be of maximum value in the high school, it must be integrated with the educational program and coordinated with the activity

calendar. To achieve this, the drama teacher must maintain the cooperation of many individuals within the high school.

The Principal and Drama

In most schools, the principal hires the drama teacher and any other
teachers who participate in theatrical activities. The principal also ap-
proves the schedule of classes offered in his school and can exercise abso-
lute control over the type and number of elective courses available to
students. He therefore has far more authority and influence regarding
drama than he has regarding English or science in his school. The principal also holds a veto power over the selection of plays and materials,
the rehearsal schedules, and all other aspects of the drama program.
It is obligatory that the drama teacher have the respect and support of
the principal.

What does a principal expect of a drama teacher? First, he wants a
teacher with a thorough knowledge of the history, literature, techniques,
crafts, and pedagogy of theatre—an expert and a specialist. It is of almost equal importance to the principal that the drama teacher have an
appreciation of the diverse educational activities and objectives of the
school. Too often the drama teacher, like the football coach, becomes so
involved in his own project that he forgets that his students have a
primary obligation to do satisfactory work in all their classes. The study
of one subject or participation in one activity should never infringe upon
a student's other classes. Nothing can cause so much resentment of the
drama teacher and damage to the drama program as taking students out
of classes for rehearsals or allowing them to use rehearsals as an excuse
for not doing homework.

Principals expect their drama teachers to be willing to assist with other
school activities which are related to their theatre specialty. Skits for
club programs, assemblies, PTA events, senior class activities, awards
banquets, and student talent shows all need the advice and guidance of
the theatre-trained teacher in the school. A drama teacher who wants
to confine his work to purely theatrical ventures will not find favor with
most principals.

Strength, tempered with tact, in dealing with students, parents, and
faculty is another quality the principal appreciates in a drama teacher.
When the drama teacher attempts to maintain high standards in his
classes and productions, there are apt to be loud complaints, on grade
day and casting day, from those who think that everyone should get an
"A" in an elective course or those who have been told repeatedly that
they have such "a natural talent" that they should be on the stage. Again
and again, the teacher-director must explain the rigorous discipline—
academic, aesthetic, and emotional—of theatre training. Most teachers

need not be able to explain the requirements of their subject discipline; the drama teacher must do it continually.

Because the drama teaching assignment is so multifaceted and highly specialized, the principal is seldom equipped to give specific aid to the teacher. He therefore needs a teacher-director who has enough initiative to find the solutions to his own problems and stay out of the principal's office.

One of the primary functions of the high school principal is public relations. His tools in good public relations are achievements by students. The principal expects the drama teacher to provide productions of plays of the highest quality. Nothing can be more effective in selling the principal on the value of drama in the school than occasional letters of commendation of a production of *Romeo and Juliet* or *The Crucible* from local citizens.

Not every principal will be aware that he should expect all these qualities in a drama teacher, but the teacher who brings them to his job will certainly gain the respect of his principal.

The Assistants to the Principal

In most schools the principal delegates much of his authority to two assistants who are called either vice principals or deans. Usually, the chief responsibility of the vice principals is maintaining student discipline. Although the drama teacher will have few occasions to call upon the vice principals in this capacity, he will be affected by other aspects of their work.

One of the vice principals is in charge of organizing the school's activity calendar, which is designed to schedule assemblies, class meetings, athletic events, plays, dances, and club meetings at the high school with as little conflict as possible. In finding dates for dramatic performances, the rehearsal facility time schedule as well as the performance dates must be considered. Few schools are equipped or staffed to present a modern dance program on Monday, a band concert on Tuesday, and a play on Wednesday, Thursday, and Friday of the same week in the same auditorium. A play presented in conflict with a football game or prom will have difficulty drawing an audience.

The vice principals are also the guardians of student morals and of good taste in the dress, language, and content of all school events. One of them is assigned to check the plays selected and be sure that they meet the standards established for the high school. For the drama teacher, discretion would seem to be the better part of valor in selecting and, where necessary, cutting the plays to be presented. If he does this well, it will soon be unnecessary to submit scripts for approval.

The liaison with the Parent Teachers Association is maintained by the vice principals who often call upon the drama teacher for programs for PTA meetings. In their capacity as sponsors of boys' and girls' activities, the vice principals often plan student assemblies. Again, they call upon the drama teacher for expert help. Finally, it is the vice principals who arrange for drama students to be excused from classes when it is necessary.

The vice principals have even more direct contact with the drama teacher than does the high school principal. They will respect the teacher-director who is skillful in controlling student behavior at after school rehearsals, as well as in the classroom.

Student enthusiasm for production work provides strong motivation to conform to any rules of conduct established by the teacher-director. First, of course, he must insist upon a no-nonsense, worklike atmosphere at all rehearsals, if he is to produce quality shows. A letter of agreement, signed by parent, student, and teacher, listing the rules of rehearsal conduct and including the rehearsal schedule, is most helpful to all concerned. (A sample of such a letter is reproduced in the Appendix.) Any student who violates the rules should be removed from the cast or crew immediately. In most cases, since his production assignment will constitute the major part of his semester's grade in the drama class, he will also fail the class. It is sometimes difficult to enforce strict rules when they are violated at the eleventh hour by a student who is acting an important role well. The director will be heartsick, and other actors will be dejected by the feeling that the show is ruined. In addition, parents of the offender may often persuade administrators to attempt to intercede to get the director to make an exception. The director who will enforce his rules in the face of outside pressure and his own reluctance to damage weeks of hard work will ultimately gain the deep respect of all concerned and strengthen his drama program.

One unbelievably complicated situation involved an uncommonly talented student body president and straight "A" student, who missed a dress rehearsal and had to be replaced in a leading role two days before the opening. Failure in the class caused his removal from the presidency. A few members of the cast threatened to withdraw if he were not reinstated. The combined pressure of the parents, the student government sponsor, the principal, and ultimately, the superintendent of schools, failed to change the decision. When I promised legal action and resignation if my actions were reversed, my decision was upheld and the show went on quite successfully with a replacement in the lead. There was even a happy ending. The following semester the student requested readmission to the drama class. He was accepted without prejudice and again cast in a leading role. He rehearsed conscientiously and earned an "A" in the class.

Skill in production organization, rehearsal scheduling, and program planning is a great asset to the drama teacher in his relationships with vice principals. Since they are concerned with the quality of all programs and with student audience conduct, they soon become aware of the caliber of the drama teacher's skills in creating and organizing performances of all kinds.

Many duties and tasks in the comprehensive high school are not specifically part of any faculty assignment. The vice principals are responsible for finding faculty members to chaperone social activities, supervise athletic events, control student behavior on the campus, and sponsor clubs. They are most appreciative of a drama teacher who will assume his share of these extra duties. For the drama teacher, it is time well-invested in good will.

As an advisor to all others who are concerned with assemblies and programs, the drama teacher can be valuable to the vice principals by helping to see that the materials presented have educational as well as entertainment value and are enhanced by effective production techniques. Often his suggestions for staging programs will make them more attractive and interesting to view. He should also be able to suggest materials suitable for a variety of occasions, as will be discussed in a later chapter.

Even the most efficient schedule of programs, concerts, assemblies, and plays in a high school can be upset by weather conditions, physical illness, emergency meetings, the U.S. mails, or a championship football team. In such instances, adaptability to emergencies and the ability to find alternate solutions becomes the drama teacher's most important requirement in the eyes of the vice principals.

The Counselor

The counselor, with the approval of the principal, is responsible for the master schedule of required and elective courses offered in the high school. The counselor is in charge of the testing and guidance program, and advises students in the selection of their classes. He determines the number of drama classes to be offered, the kind of drama classes to be encouraged, and the kind of students to be enrolled in these classes. The counselor is genuinely interested in the educational and personal welfare of the students, and he usually knows more about the qualities of each teacher and the content of each course than anyone else.

Minimally, the counselor expects a drama program that interests and benefits the students involved in it. He wants the drama teacher to be interested in the development of students and to make use of the available guidance and testing data. Often, drama teachers must teach other subjects, and the counselor expects them to be proficient in those classes. Most of all, because the nature of the subject requires the drama teacher to know and teach his students individually, the counselor expects him to assist in guiding both the problem students of the school and those who are exceptionally gifted.

Although it may be unfortunate that the counselor has no criteria for the drama program except that it interests and benefits the students, this attitude at least gives the drama teacher the opportunity to develop any kind of program he is able to create. If his program becomes a re-creation camp for lazy students to acquire credit without homework, that kind of student will be advised to take drama. If the program develops into a pseudo-psychological group therapy meeting, students who are misfits will be enrolled in drama. If the classes become an exciting creative and intellectual experience, students who want that kind of challenge will take drama. The counselor will usually accept any of these common patterns in drama classes, as long as they interest a number of students. After all, the counselor must provide a class schedule for all kinds of students, and the nature of the individual classes determines which students are assigned to which classes. This is not to say that the counselor would not prefer to encourage a quality program in drama. He would. There are enough thriving drama programs that are merely recreational, however, to support the claim that a drama program can exist only as a dumping ground for intractable students. After a year or two, the drama teacher gets the kind of students he wants and deserves in his classes.

The Faculty

Any sponsor of a club or class who wishes to present a banquet program or an assembly may call upon the drama teacher for help. In responding to this call, the drama teacher will not only create a reservoir of good will toward himself and his program but may also help develop greater respect for the arts and crafts of theatre.

The faculty will come to respect and support a drama program that deals with ideas and is more concerned with values and education than with entertainment.

It may not be entirely logical, but once a student becomes identified with dramatic activities, faculty members tend to assume that the drama teacher is responsible for all phases of that student's schooling. They will request the drama teacher's assistance in getting a student to do his geometry homework or to keep quiet in history class. The drama teacher certainly does have an opportunity to influence his students' behavior, and perhaps his role as teacher gives him a moral obligation to do what he can to improve the behavior of his students in all situations.

It is natural that most teachers feel that their subject discipline is vitally important to students and therefore every minute of every class period is essential. They tend to resent any kind of interruption (from daily bulletins to office summons) that infringes on their time. They are especially disturbed if students miss class because of rehearsal for a play or an assembly, which seems to them of no real educational value.

It is astounding that some drama teachers are so zealously dedicated to theatre that they fail to understand—much less to respect—this same zeal on the part of other teachers! The first step is to respect the dedication of other teachers to their disciplines. The second, is for the drama teacher to attempt to gain respect and understanding for his discipline. He can do this by cooperating with other teachers, as suggested in various places in this chapter, and by educating the faculty and students to the values of the arts in education, as outlined elsewhere in this text.

The first law of self preservation for the drama teacher, as stated earlier is, never do a senior play. The second law of self preservation is, never take students out of classes for rehearsals. All rehearsals should be held during the drama class or after school. The only time students need to miss other classes is on the day of performance when, if they are to get into costumes and make up, they must obviously arrive at the theatre ahead of the audience.

In addition to the general support of the faculty, the drama teacher needs the active assistance of teachers with specific skills. Sometimes these teachers are assigned to help with the production program, and other times they must be persuaded to volunteer. In either case, the drama teacher must respect their talents, appreciate their contributions, and court their favor.

Art teachers are needed most often to assist with the drama program. Their talents and skills are most obviously needed in the design of scenery and decorations for the stage, in the selection of style and colors, and in the execution of these designs. Art teachers can also be helpful in designing and producing printed materials needed to publicize and produce plays, such as posters, mailers, and programs. In some high schools, art departments offer classes in stage design and in advertising art, and art students will work on art problems related to the drama programs as part of their assigned classwork. In most schools, however, the drama teacher will have to solicit the help of art teachers, until they can jointly develop appropriate art classes.

Art teachers appreciate the opportunities that participation in the drama program gives their students to display their work for the public. The group nature of stage design and decoration offers an excellent balance in the training of art students, who work primarily on individual projects. It is important that the director be specific about the mood, style, interpretation, and obligatory physical requirements of the play. The art teacher will know better than the teacher-director how to translate these factors into plastic and visual language and will work most willingly if his expertise is respected.

Of equal importance to the production of plays in the high school is the stage crew sponsor, who is usually an industrial arts teacher. He is apt to know electricity, carpentry, and electronics but seldom understands the application of these skills to the theatre. The stage crew should be responsible for the construction of the scenery, which is designed and painted under the supervision of the art teacher. To bridge the gap between the artists and the mechanics, the teacher-director may have to prepare scale drawings of all of the needed construction, if the other two teachers are either unwilling or unable to do this. It should be noted that the tendency of industrial arts teachers who are assigned to stagecraft work is to do the job better than it needs to be done in some respects. In both materials and workmanship, their standards may be too high. In some instances, flats have been constructed of oak with glued, tongue and groove joints, and stairsteps, which would support elephants but could not be lifted by four strong men. Scenery for a high school play does not have to withstand a two-year national tour and must usually be shifted by manpower rather than by stage machinery. The stage crew teacher often needs advice about materials and techniques of stage construction from the drama teacher.

Even more complex are the problems of stage lighting, for which the stage crew instructor is responsible. Except in those rare, wealthy school districts, where trained theatre technicians are employed, the drama teacher must be proficient in stage lighting. If he makes a detailed light plot, including instruments, gels, positions, intensity, and cues, the stage crew will enjoy executing it. In a very short time, if the teacher-director establishes a good relationship with the stage crew teacher, he will find that full responsibilities for the technical aspects of production can be assumed by the stage crew. If it is not possible to find an industrial arts teacher willing to learn theatre techniques, the drama teacher may either attempt to persuade an art teacher to teach stagecraft or do it himself.

The teacher-director often finds expert and willing assistance from the faculty in selecting music and costuming. Every show can be enhanced by appropriate music for an overture and intermissions, and many require internal music. Music teachers can suggest materials and offer a student ensemble or recorded music for plays. Some may even compose music for school plays. A drama teacher and music teacher have many common interests and problems in the high school. If they view their arts as complementary rather than competitive, both theatre and music will thrive.

Although costumes are often rented from commercial concerns, there are occasions when it is more economical to make them. The home economics teachers can be called upon to supervise students in constructing costumes.

Unique requirements of individual productions may cause the drama teacher to call upon members of the faculty whose professional or avocational interests qualify them as authorities. Foreign language passages appear in many plays, and language teachers can train student actors to say them correctly. Experts in sign language, acrobatics, dance, religious traditions, national customs, fencing, and firearms, can be found on most high school faculties. Their advice can give authenticity to the production. The faculty is a far more lively, interesting, and readily available source of information than many directors realize. Tap it!

Results of Good Relationships

The teacher-director who respects and understands the responsibilities of his colleagues and teaches them to respect and understand drama in education will make his own job easier and his productions better.

The principal, in consideration of the after school hours spent by the drama teacher, may lighten his teaching load during school hours. Once the principal understands the value of drama in the school, he will increase the number and kinds of drama and related classes in the curriculum. When the principal learns to respect the taste and judgment of the teacher-director, he will relax his censorship of materials.

The counselors respond to an educationally sound drama program in several ways. First, they encourage students with high intelligence to enroll in drama as an enrichment of their cultural background. Their encouragement results in a greater student demand for drama and in more drama classes. Once counselors understand the individual nature of much of the instruction in a drama class, they cooperate in limiting the size of each class. Counselors will also cooperate in developing new classes in drama, play production, design, and stagecraft, if the drama teacher offers them an outline of the curriculum for such classes. Where mastery of certain information and skills is important to success in some drama classes, the counselor will help the drama teacher establish prerequisites for admission to these classes. In his capacity as advisor to both the principal and the students, the counselor's attitude largely determines the quality and quantity of the drama program.

Assistance from the teachers of art, industrial arts, and other faculty members in solving some of the production problems of high school theatre will certainly improve its quality. Productions of good quality generate interest in the whole area of the theatre among faculty as well as students. Often this interest is manifested by the use of school plays as teaching devices in other classes. This will be discussed in Chapter 8.

The successful drama teacher is the one who is aware of his limitations as well as his abilities. He knows that his job cannot be done alone, and he seeks the advice, aid, and cooperation of his colleagues. He offers his help in other school activities and plans his production program with careful consideration of the other activities within the high school.

CHAPTER 5

Community Relations

The community relations and public image of the high school are affected by every contact between the school or its representatives and students, parents, businesses, or citizens. Certainly, the drama program is more visible to the community than most of the high school's departments; those working in high school theatre must be particularly sensitive to all aspects of community relationships.

In order to produce plays, the teacher-director must call upon the community for numerous services and supplies, as well as for publicity and an audience. Drama becomes a business as well as an educational activity of the high school when the total production picture is considered.

Reciprocity Between Drama and Community

The drama teacher's most frequent community contacts are with business establishments. He will need the services of a printer to produce tickets, advertising brochures, posters, and programs for plays. Good relationships can be established by asking the printer's advice on layout, paper stock, and the use of color, and by prompt payment of bills. The result should be quality printing at minimum costs, because the printer will be able to display pride in his work and interest in his community school.

The purchase of materials needed for play production should be made, whenever possible, through local businesses. Every play will require a few hundred dollars' worth of paint, lumber, hardware, fabric, and miscellaneous items for properties. It is important that the drama teacher call on these local merchants personally to establish the initial contact and develop rapport between the businesses and the school. Later a student representative will be treated with courtesy when he goes to the shop and says, "Mr. Smith, my drama teacher, asked me to get a price on three-inch, ball-bearing casters." An occasional telephone call or visit from the drama teacher will keep the relationships cordial and the services excellent.

In return for patronage and as a consequence of good relationships, local businessmen will aid the school drama program by displaying posters advertising the play, by purchasing advertising in the playbill, and by buying or distributing tickets to the school's productions.

Parents are more closely associated with the drama program than any other group within the community, and their attitudes affect the success of theatrical activities. The drama program provides their children with activities that are both educational and recreational. It provides parents and the community with worthwhile cultural events. When they become aware of its contributions, parents are grateful that a drama program exists in the local high school. Parents can support the drama program by attending productions, encouraging their children to participate in it, and helping to assemble properties, costumes, and furniture for school plays.

Every community has a number of civic service organizations like Lions, Kiwanis, Rotary, Women's Club, and the Chamber of Commerce. Each of these groups is organized for the purpose of supporting any activity that contributes to the welfare and well-being of the citizens of the community. By producing plays appropriate for community audiences, the high school drama department offers a community service worthy of the support of these civic clubs. The resourceful teacher-director who calls upon civic organizations will find them willing to publicize school plays at their meetings and even to sell tickets to their members.

All drama teachers seek the aid of local newspapers in publicizing their plays, but few seem to be aware that the school drama program provides a valuable service to the press. Community and school news items, which offer names and photographs of local people, are a major factor in promoting reader interest for the newspapers. Although newspapers seldom come to the high school to cover drama activities, they are always willing to print material sent to them in good form. News items about the play should include names of student actors and crews and should be written in journalistic style. Photographs should be close-ups and have attached a caption identifying the subjects. If the stories have interest and variety, newspapers will carry several items about each production or program of the drama department.

Effect of Good Community Relations

Attention to all of these facets of community relationships will pay dividends not only in good will but also in larger audiences for school plays. Larger audiences produce greater revenue and therefore a larger budget for the production of school plays.

The growth of the community audience for the high school's plays can contribute to community pride in the school and to a greater respect for the drama program. The fact that the high school principal's support of drama is affected by the attitude of parents and community has been mentioned in the preceding chapter. Perhaps it should also be pointed out that the drama program's association with the community is a prime factor in the attitude of members of the board of education toward drama in the schools. In most districts, members of the board are elected by the public and are therefore sensitive to community attitudes toward every aspect of public education. Boards of education bear the ultimate responsibility for the expenditure of school funds as well as for the curriculum. Although they seek the advice of school administrators, the decisions of boards of education are strongly influenced by community opinion.

In order to develop and maintain good community relationships the drama teacher must keep their importance in mind when selecting materials for production as well as when contacting individuals in the community. He must certainly be aware that the most important tool of good community relationships is a good play—well acted, well directed, and well produced. The play cannot be considered a complete success, however, until it is well-attended by a community as well as a student audience. Community attendance at school plays is the goal of the drama department's community relations program.

Many of the factors involved in obtaining a community audience are discussed in Chapter 6.

Publicity
and Promotion
of Drama

Although the teacher and the huckster may be at opposite idealogical poles, the drama teacher will find it necessary to learn and to practice some of the huckster's crafts in order to attract an audience for high school plays. It is as true that a play does not exist until an audience sees it, as it is that a tree falling in the forest makes no sound until an ear hears it. In addition to the aesthetic requirement that plays have audiences, there is a practical need for a paying audience for high school productions. The subsidy of theatre in public education is usually limited to paying the salary of the teacher-director and providing the auditorium or theatre without charge. All production costs—scripts, royalties, scenery, lighting, sound, costumes, make-up, props, and printing—must be paid by box-office receipts. In order to survive, the high school theatre must have enough publicity and promotion to bring a paying audience to its productions.

Publicity and Promotion Personnel

A drama teacher is not likely to have either the time or the talents required to do a good job of publicizing his production. He must nevertheless be responsible for the overall planning of each publicity campaign and for seeking the cooperation of the school personnel who will execute the plans.

Many large high schools have a faculty member assigned as a publicity director. If such a person is available, the drama director need only provide him with the information and materials for community publicity. If the school does not have a publicity director, the drama teacher will either have to do the job himself or find a volunteer. In fact, one of the most heartening aspects of teaching is that there are so many faculty colleagues willing to help with any worthwhile project. An English teacher is apt to be the best qualified person to help with publicity.

An effective publicity campaign will require the specialized skills of several others among the school's personnel: the journalism teacher, the advertising art teacher, the printer, the photographer, the financial manager, the student government sponsor, and the business education teacher. It is advisable to appoint one of the better drama students to assist the drama teacher with publicity and maintain communications among the various people involved in publicizing and promoting the play.

Publicity Tools and Materials

A publicity summary, prepared by the director and his student publicity chairman, is a good device for starting and planning publicity. The publicity summary should be prepared and distributed to all concerned personnel six or eight weeks prior to the production and should include the following information:

> title of play
> dates of performances
> admission prices
> brief résumé of plot
> biographical sketch of playwright
> character descriptions and cast names
> student production staff
> faculty production staff
> interesting or unusual biographical data of actors, director, or staff
> suggested schedule for publicity campaign

From this summary, those responsible for each part of the publicity and promotion can obtain the information they need without frequent conferences with the director. (A sample publicity summary appears in the Appendix.)

Early in the rehearsal period, photographs of the cast in rehearsal should be taken so that prints may be sent to the community and school newspapers. Since it is seldom possible to have costumes for these photographs, student actors should be asked to wear "date" rather than "school" clothes for the pictures. Pictures can be made more interesting by running scenes and shooting bits of action than by lining actors up in artificial poses. The photographer should be onstage, close to the actors, and only two or three actors should be in each picture. Care needs to be taken to assure pictures with good black and white contrast so that they will reproduce clearly in a newspaper. The pictures should be printed on 8" × 10" glossy stock, and a typewritten caption, giving the names of the play, the actors, the school, and the dates of performance should be pasted to the back of each picture.

A list of additional publicity materials that must be prepared, with a notation of who is responsible for each, may be helpful.

> Posters—Design: art department
> > Production: print shop or art department
>
> Postal cards—Design: art department
> > Production: print shop
>
> Handbills—Design: art department
> > Production: business departments
>
> Letters to schools—Copy: drama director
> > Production: business department
>
> Tickets—Copy: financial manager
> > Production: print shop
>
> Ticket sales slips—Copy: financial manager
> > Production: print shop

Use of Publicity Materials

Using the information contained in the publicity summary, the school's publicity director and the student newspaper sponsor should begin to publicize the play in the community and the school press five to six weeks before the production dates. The first news item might announce the selection of the play and give information on the play and playwright. The next might announce the cast chosen. Subsequent news and feature stories might deal with interesting aspects of the set design or construction, rehearsal problems or amusing incidents, individual actors, and so on. Appropriate photographs can be used with some of these stories. Three or four news items concerning the play being produced at the high school should appear in each available newspaper prior to the show. It is important in maintaining good relationships with the press that identical news releases not be sent to all papers. Each outlet should receive different photographs and stories featuring different aspects of the production.

The journalism teacher and his trained students should be enlisted to prepare materials for the newspaper. If such expert help is not available, the drama teacher can instruct some of his own students in some of the elementary rules of journalistic writing. The first paragraph, preferably in one sentence, should answer the questions: Who? What? When? Where? Why? Subsequent paragraphs should be of decreasing importance so that the editor with limited space can cut a final paragraph or two without rewriting the story or omitting essential information. All items submitted should be typewritten, double-spaced, and clearly identified, as follows:

> To: Name of appropriate editor
>   Name of newspaper
> From: Name of writer
>   Name of school
>   Address and telephone
> Re: Subject of release
> Date: When written
>   For immediate release

Posters, attractively designed and containing some kind of illustration, may be printed either in the print shop or in the art department by the silk screen process. A crew of half a dozen students, selected from drama classes, business classes, or student government, can distribute fifty to one hundred posters to local merchants and businessmen for display.

The teacher-director should develop a mailing list, made up of past patrons of school plays and of school alumni interested in drama. Postal cards, announcing each play, can be addressed by a business or a drama class and mailed two or three weeks before each production. In addition to this mailing list, members of the cast and crew may be given postal cards to send to personal friends.

Mimeographed handbills, which give information about the play to be presented and how to obtain tickets, can be mailed to parents or distributed at other school events, like athletic games, band concerts, and PTA meetings, which are attended by adults in the community.

Students from the business department can type letters of invitation to drama teachers in nearby schools, members of the board of education, and other interested individuals. These should also be mailed two or three weeks before the production. Although few of those invited will attend, the letters are worth sending because of the good will they create.

Student speakers, either from speech or drama classes, may be sent to meetings of local service clubs to publicize the play and to urge club members to attend. In some cases, members of the cast may present brief scenes from the play to stimulate interest. Student speakers may also take play tickets with them to sell to those interested in attending. It is important that these presentations emphasize the school's desire to have community members attend the play, rather than contribute financial support by buying tickets they will not use. It is almost too easy to pressure members of a service club into buying tickets, and this kind of pressure will eventually create ill will for the drama program. From the viewpoint of student actors, it is just as disheartening to play to an empty house for which all the tickets were sold, as to play to an empty house for which the tickets were not sold.

To promote ticket sales among members of the student body, a brief teaser scene from the play may be presented at an assembly a couple of weeks before the production. The scene should be selected to stimulate interest in the play without revealing too much of the plot. If possible, it should be presented in costume and make-up, but without the scenery of the play.

All publicity and promotional activity is wasted unless it is supplemented by a strong ticket sales campaign. Since it is not practical to issue actual tickets to student salesmen, a ticket sales slip is a helpful device. These slips can be printed in large numbers and given to student salesmen. Each slip should be numbered, have a stub with the same number, and contain the following information: name of play, price of admission, name of salesmen, number of tickets purchased, total amount paid. The student salesman fills out the slip and stub, collects the money for tickets, and gives the slip to the purchaser. He then takes the stub and money to the school's finance office, picks up the tickets, and returns them to the purchaser.

The greatest problem, of course, is finding a group of good student salesmen. Those schools whose business education departments offer a class in salesmanhip may find an easy solution to this problem. Other schools must find an interested teacher, club, or class willing to undertake the project.

The responsibility for publicity and promotion, added to the problems of directing and producing a play, is burdensome. The director can lighten this burden by careful planning and by enlisting the aid of other faculty members. The final responsibility for follow-up and execution of the plans, however, remains with the drama director. If the campaign succeeds it will pay dividends in larger, more receptive audiences, larger budgets, and greater respect for the high school drama program.

CHAPTER 7

Assembly Programs and Entertainments

In addition to his activities as a director of plays, the high school drama teacher is usually required to produce assembly programs and various other kinds of entertainments. The successful secondary school director must therefore be more versatile, more resourceful, and more creative than the successful commercial director. He has less expert assistance, and he is responsible for a wider variety of theatrical activities. The commercial director is surrounded by specially trained colleagues: a producer, writers, costumer, set designer, lighting technician, business manager, publicist, choreographer, and many others. The high school director must play all these roles himself, either alternately or simultaneously. The commercial director often becomes a specialist in one kind of production, such as musical comedy, Shakespeare, drama, situation comedy, or variety shows, whereas the high school director may be required to direct each kind of production.

Kinds of Programs

It may be a considerable shock to the teacher who accepts a job as a drama teacher to learn that he is expected to produce dozens of assemblies, which are entirely different in content and format from theatre. Perhaps the best way to comprehend the scope of these activities is to list typical assemblies presented annually in many high schools.

Traditionally, major holidays are commemorated with assemblies.

Thanksgiving, Christmas, Easter, Washington's Birthday, Lincoln's Birthday, Veteran's Day are celebrated. Brotherhood Week, United Nations Week, Bill of Rights Week, and others are often added to the list. For example, the author was once requested to hold an assembly for Susan B. Anthony Day! Obviously, the age and sophistication of high school students prohibits the use of the Pilgrim's feast, Santa Claus, the cherry tree myth, and the Easter Bunny! Fear that the school may be accused of violating the First Amendment further restricts the selection of materials for some of these assemblies. One of the *Up the Down Staircase* delights of teaching drama in recent years has become reading the annual administrative directive on nonreligious Christmas programs. In some schools, it has been decided that reading from the Bible is religious, but that singing Handel's music is *not* religious!

Student activities beget another group of programs, including student government campaign assemblies, awards assemblies, class meetings, pep assemblies, and talent shows. The task of making the first four of these interesting and the last two tasteful often falls to the drama teacher.

Several kinds of programs are associated with the senior class and graduation—class day, vesper services, senior concerts, and commencement exercises are among the options. Which programs are chosen depends upon the tradition of the individual high school.

Finally, many high schools have fund-raising programs for a variety of causes. The need for athletic or band equipment, for student group trips, or for other equipment and activities, and contributions to the United Fund, Red Cross, and other community groups are occasions for fund-raising assemblies. The drama teacher should be delighted to help provide these programs so that he will not have to use the production of plays for fund raising!

This list of more than twenty-five different programs, many of which occur annually in every school, does not include programs staged by the school's performing arts groups—choir, glee club, modern dance, band, and orchestra—that may also require assistance from the drama teacher. The drama teacher is expected to see that all these events not only serve their respective utilitarian ends, but also are both interesting and educationally valuable.

Assembly Organization, Materials, and Direction

It would be impossible to enumerate the specific procedure and content of each kind of high school program, but some general suggestions may help in solving the problems associated with them.

The first step in preparing any program or assembly is to analyze the problems it presents. A list of questions may help do this quickly.

What is the purpose of this program?

How has it been presented in the past?

Does it need improvement?

Can it be made more interesting?

Can it be done more efficiently?

Is a new format desirable?

Who are to be the participants?

Guided by the answers to these questions, the drama teacher can organize a plan for the production and presentation of each assembly.

The plan should begin with content—a list of the items on the program in the order of their presentation. Next, the materials to be used for the program, such as scripts, music, speeches, and recordings, should be gathered. When these materials have been assembled, the participants in each part of the program can be selected or assigned. It is important at this point that a clear division of duties and responsibilities be made. Who does what? When must he do each thing? Often, participants in assemblies are not acquainted with the process and disciplines of public performance, and their specific jobs must be defined for them in detail.

A schedule of the rehearsals required to prepare the assembly should be part of the drama teacher's plan. For most assembly programs, segments can be rehearsed separately, with the entire group coming together only once or twice for a final rehearsal before the performance. If all of this seems obvious to the drama teacher, experience in a high school will soon show him that it is not obvious to most of the students and faculty who participate in assemblies. If not told to rehearse separately, they may arrive at the final rehearsal saying, "Here I am. Now what do you want me to do?" They have not even looked at their script since it was handed to them!

Finally, the plan for an assembly should include the assistance of other faculty members. If the program includes musical numbers, for example, a music teacher may be asked to guide rehearsals for that segment. If the program involves large numbers of students, faculty supervision may be required. In some cases, it may be necessary to plan where each group is to assemble, in what order they line up, through which door they enter the auditorium, and so on.

The drama teacher's planning and organization of assemblies will not only improve their quality but also conserve the time and energy of all concerned.

Many school programs, particularly commencement exercises, include original speeches prepared and delivered by students with no specific speech training. If the faculty does not include a public speaking teacher, the drama teacher should try to improve the quality of these speeches.

Although his theatrical training qualifies him to assist students in the effective delivery of speeches, it usually does not prepare him to guide students in writing their speeches. There are many textbooks on speech to which a drama teacher may refer for techniques of speech preparation. Among the most useful is Alan H. Monroe's *Principles of Speech,*[1] which offers a relatively simple method of organizing and writing speeches that is clearly and concisely explained. Monroe calls his method of organization a motivated sequence. It abandons the traditional three-step outline of introduction, body, and conclusion, in favor of a five-step outline of (1) attention, (2) need, (3) satisfaction, (4) visualization, and (5) action. Monroe's method of organization helps the student state his ideas more clearly and logically.

The problems of finding interesting and meaningful materials for various assemblies are not so easily solved as those of improving speech techniques. The idea of a nonreligious Easter program is very funny until one faces the question of what to do for that program. In general, the packaged scripts for special occasion assembly programs, which are offered to the drama teacher through numerous catalogues from obscure publishers are not worth the cost of obtaining them or the time required to examine them. Original programs, collected from standard sources of history and literature, are far more satisfactory than prepared program scripts. A Christmas progam which contains readings of *The Gift of the Magi,* and *The Littlest Angel,* for example, along with selections by the school chorus, is both entertaining and enjoyable. A Veteran's Day assembly, composed of excerpts from speeches of wartime Presidents, interspersed with martial and popular music of each period, can be both informative and interesting.

School libraries are rich with well-written materials—poetry, essays, editorials, short stories, speeches, and historical and biographical incidents—which can be selected to suit almost any occasion or theme and adapted for presentation in an assembly.

Materials selected from these sources can be staged in a variety of simple but interesting ways. The stage can be decorated with colorful screens, emblems, risers, or set pieces. Student readers can be costumed and placed on different levels in various areas of the stage and pinspotted for their individual readings. Appropriate musical bridges or musical background, either from records or from a guitar or organ, can be used to enhance the readings.

The commercially successful and exciting productions of *Spoon River Anthology* and *Under Milkwood* illustrate the kinds of production techniques and literary materials that can be used in high school assemblies. Finding and staging materials for assembly programs is a stimulating

[1] Alan H. Monroe, *Principles of Speech,* Rev. brief ed. (Chicago: Scott, Foresman & Company, 1951).

challenge to the creative abilities of the drama teacher, as well as a welcome opportunity to expand the cultural background of the student audience. Working with assembly programs in this manner gives the high school teacher-director another way to show the valuable contribution that the theatre arts can make to education.

Variety and Talent Shows

Although many drama teachers and school administrators abhor their existence, variety shows are often tolerated because no one knows how to eliminate them. They persist because they offer opportunities for wide student participation, and because their popularity with students makes them an excellent means of fund-raising. Many large schools have substituted musical comedies, for which the music teachers are primarily responsible, with the drama teacher assisting in blocking and staging, for the musical shows. However, the high cost, both in money and man hours, of producing musicals makes them a questionable alternative.

If the variety or talent show still exists, it usually becomes the drama teacher's responsibility, and he should try to produce as good a show as possible. The organizational techniques discussed earlier in this chapter will be essential in the coordination of a variety show. The cooperation of the music teachers in assessing potential musical talent, and later in rehearsing that talent, is of great importance to the quality of a variety show. In some cases, the music teacher may be able to form a pit combo to accompany the various numbers in the show. A committee of students with experience in drama and stagecraft can constitute the production staff for the variety show. In many cases, a student director may be chosen to work with the drama teacher and relieve him of many production details.

To avoid creating a poor imitation of *the Ed Sullivan Show* in which a master of ceremonies introduces Mary to sing, John to tap dance, Harry to imitate Marlon Brando, and George to play a drum solo, it is wise to select a theme or core idea for the show. The theme should be publicized so auditioning students can select materials that suit the core idea. For example, the theme might be "A Trip to Paris," "South of the Border," "Around the World," or "The Gay Nineties."

The selection of participants in a school variety show is usually done through try-outs, which are open to all students. Some suggestions on how to manage these auditions may be helpful. The drama teacher is wise to have a committee to help select the performers rather than take the full responsibility himself. This committee should include a music teacher, the student production staff, the drama teacher, and if possible, a school administrator. Before try-outs begin, the probable number of performers to be selected for each category in the show should be determined. Such an estimate will prevent a show that consists of twenty folk-singing guitarists and ten rock-and-roll bands. It will save time and make selection easier if each category—vocalists, instrumentalists, dancers, comedians—is auditioned separately.

Once the performers and numbers have been selected, the student director and several student writers can be put to work deciding upon the order of their appearance in the show and inventing and writing continuity material to unify the production around the selected theme. From students who have tried out or from drama students, two or three actors may be assigned to the roles in the continuity. A unifying device does much to make the variety show more interesting to the audience. Perhaps it should be mentioned that in addition to being a good method of fund raising, the variety show contributes greatly to student morale and school spirit—important elements in any high school.

Student Audience Behavior

Since the era when children were to be seen and not heard has evolved into an era in which children must be allowed uninhibited self-expression, some plans must be made to teach students how to behave properly as members of an audience. In addition to changes in social attitudes toward children, there have been radical changes in the physical environment in which they have been reared. The present generation of teenagers has teethed on television and grown up to the tune of electronically amplified sound. Thus they have learned not to hear, not to concentrate, not to pay attention to what goes on around them, unless its beat is so strong that it reaches them through their bodies as well as through their ears. In addition to this conditioning, their sub- and early teens have been spent at the movies, where they gather with friends to socialize and picnic while they ignore the oversized TV picture and the overamplified sound track.

Part of the task of presenting assemblies at the high school is teaching the audience to stay in their seats, to listen, and to refrain from commenting to those around them. The student audience may even need to be told that quiet attention is what is expected of them in the auditorium. They may need to be told that applause is an accepted and appropriate means of showing their appreciation for what they have seen on the stage and that whistling, yelling, and stamping are accepted only in the stadium.

Fortunately, except for the few rebels who deliberately attempt to disrupt any school activity, high school students are willing to cooperate once they understand the rules of the game. It is wise therefore, either by program notes, the school bulletin, or an opening announcement, to let students know what kind of program they are to see. It may also be a good idea to have student ushers quickly remove from the assembly those students who choose to be discourteous.

General restlessness or rudeness on the part of a high school student audience can usually be attributed to the quality of the program being offered to them. If it is dull, if it insults their intelligence and maturity, if it is ineptly performed, the student audience will squirm in their seats, shuffle their feet, and guffaw at mistakes. The correction for this kind of audience behavior lies not in tighter audience discipline, but rather in improvement of the assembly program.

School assemblies, programs, and entertainments offer the drama teacher challenges and opportunities that can bring him great satisfaction both as artist and as educator.

CHAPTER 8

Audience Education

Although the education of the student audience is seldom listed as a primary reason for the inclusion of classes in drama and the production of plays at the high school, audience education is potentially the area of greatest challenge and widest opportunity for the high school teacher-director. Through the production of plays, he becomes a teacher to every student in his school. By the nature of the theatre arts, the drama teacher can contribute to the learning of the student audience both intellectually and emotionally. The understandings acquired through emotional experience, through empathy, are the most lasting and influential forms of learning. Empathy is the language of the theatre, which communicates more directly, clearly, and permanently to its audience than the language of words. Audience education encompasses not only answers to the questions, "What is theatre, and how do I behave toward it?" but more importantly, "What is life, and how do I behave toward it?" Viewed in this context, audience education becomes the most important aspect of theatre in the school.

Audience Preparation Through Classes

The fact that high school students may have no knowledge of how to behave as members of a theatre audience has already been discussed in Chapter 7. The suggestions made concerning behavior in assemblies may need to be reinforced to prepare students to see a play. In presenting a play to a student audience, as in presenting an assembly, the best device for audience control is a production of high quality.

A play, however, is a more complex experience than an assembly. The play can be more fully appreciated and more educationally valuable if students are given some advance classroom preparation for seeing it. The amount of preparation that may be necessary or useful depends, of course, upon the particular play to be presented. If, heaven forfend, the school is producing *Ten Little Indians* or *Arsenic and Old Lace,* no advance audience preparation is necessary or perhaps possible. The following discussion of audience preparation is based on the assumption that the plays presented to high school students will have educational significance and will be selected by criteria similar to those suggested in Chapter 13.

Because dramatic literature is part of the curriculum in most English courses, English teachers are almost always willing to cooperate in preparing the student audience to see a play. Some plays may relate directly to other subjects taught in the school and thereby motivate other teachers to assist in this preparation. These teachers will need some materials and suggestions from the teacher-director. Several extra copies should be obtained for circulation among teachers who will be preparing their classes to see the play. Before these scripts are circulated, it is helpful if the director indicates any cuts or revisions he plans to make. The director may also wish to give teachers a statement about what he feels to be important in the play selected. A number of other aids, which can best be described by giving examples, may be offered to the teachers.

The following two bulletins were issued by Guy Raner, Chairman of the Social Studies Department at Canoga Park High School.

December 6, 1955

Memo to U.S. History I Teachers
Subject: Play—*The Crucible* by
           Arthur Miller

I would like to urge that some class attention be devoted to the subject of this play—the Salem Witch Trials—before the performance, if possible, so the students will be more familiar with the proceedings.

This is the first time that the play has been directly concerned with the subject matter of U.S. History I, and it is an attempt worthy of our strongest support. Arthur Miller, as you perhaps know, has won every playwriting prize: the Pulitzer Prize in 1949 for *Death of a Salesman,* the Drama Critics Circle Award, and the Antoinette Perry Award. *The Crucible* has received rave notices and has already been translated into several foreign languages. This is the first time a high school group has presented the play, and it has been selected by the American Educational Theatre Association for presentation (with its Canoga High School cast) at its national convention on December 29th. So we not only have a play which ties in with our course of study, but also a recognized modern masterpiece in the drama field.

Some local sources of information about the witch trials include the following from books available in class sets in the book room, which would be of interest to students either before or after they see the play:

Cook-Miller-Loban, *Adventures in Appreciation,* 2nd ed. (New York: Harcourt, Brace & World, Inc., 1943), pp. 334–42.

Stephen Vincent Benét, "We Aren't Superstitious." A complete account of the witch trial proceedings.

Commager and Nevins, editors, *Heritage of America* (Readings in American History), Chapter 9: "The Puritans Hunt Witches in Salem," (Boston: D. C. Heath & Co., 1949), pp. 47–53. Three contemporary accounts are included, one by Cotton Mather.

April 17, 1956

Memo to Social Studies Teachers

The play this year will be *The Skin of Our Teeth* by Thornton Wilder, which won the Pulitzer Prize in 1943. The original New York production, directed by Elia Kazan (who later won an Academy Award for his direction of *On the Waterfront*), starred Fredric March, Florence Eldridge, and Tallulah Bankhead.

The play, a comedy, requires very careful attention from the audience if the greatest enjoyment and understanding are to be gained. It uses a good many theatrical tricks you may not be used to, for example, at times, an actor will turn to the audience and begin explaining part of the play, or the stage manager will walk in and explain something to the audience or to an actor, or new persons will wander on to the stage and explain that the regular actors got sick and they are replacing them. The object of the play is to present an optimistic history of mankind, showing that even through an ice age, a flood, or a war, somehow mankind manages to survive, by the skin of his teeth.

The name of the main character is George Antrobus—a name obviously derived from the Greek word, Anthropos, meaning "human being" or "man." Chronology (time sequence) is thrown to the winds in this play, with a dinosaur and a mammoth appearing together in the first act, when in fact the dinosaur became extinct several million years before the mammoth appeared. They are introduced to show that while the ice ages may have killed dinosaurs and mammoths, man survived. The time of the first act may be vaguely located as somewhere between yesterday in New Jersey, the maximum of the fourth Glacial Age, about 50,000 years ago, and in it George manages to send his wife a telegram explaining that he has invented the wheel, the alphabet, and arithmetic.

It has been suggested that some students might not be familiar with certain references in the play, so here is a little quiz to see if YOU can identify or define the following names, phrases, and terms:

1. Adam
2. Eve
3. Genesis 2:18
4. A & P
5. Ice Age
6. Mammoth
7. Dinosaur
8. Cain
9. Moses
10. Blind man with guitar, named Homer
11. Ten Commandments

12. Abel

13. Plagues

14. Charlatan

15. Jeremiah

16. Phi Beta Kappa

17. "Take these animals into the boat, two of each kind."

18. Plato

19. Aristotle

20. Spinoza

Teachers who gave this quiz were somewhat shocked by the results—most students couldn't even identify Moses. Because of this alarming absence of background, the following bulletin was prepared and distributed.

The Skin of Our Teeth

The following is additional information which I hope you will use in discussing the forthcoming production of *The Skin of Our Teeth* with your classes. I have attempted to define certain literary, historical, legendary, and Biblical allusions contained in this play in terms of their application to the story and theme. This device should enhance the students' enjoyment, appreciation, and (you'll pardon the expression) education.

Notes on the play: The Skin of Our Teeth

SIGNIFICANCE OF TITLE: We—the human race—repeatedly narrowly escaping annihilation, by the skin of our teeth, yet we do survive.

THEME: "The people will live on. The learning and blundering people will live on. . . . The people so peculiar in renewal and comeback, you can't laugh off their capacity to take it."

—Carl Sandburg

PURPOSE: To reassure us that mankind is not only capable but also worthy of survival at a time when civilization seems to be on the brink of destruction. To offer hope for and faith in the future.

METHOD: In order to achieve his purpose and illustrate his theme, Thornton Wilder divides his play into three acts—Ice Age, Great Flood, War—in each of which the annihilation of mankind seems inevitable. However, in each crisis man finds the incentive and strength to survive the catastrophe and continue his struggle toward perfection.

TYPE: Comedy. The play may be so classified by reason of both the resolution of the plot and the treatment of the theme. By classic definition, a comedy is a play in which the protagonist (in this case, Mr. Antrobus, representing mankind) is ultimately victorious. Following the contemporary customs of the theatre, comedy is also amusing and light in mood and style.

SUMMARY: Just as man has often accomplished the apparently impossible, so Mr. Wilder has accomplished the apparently impossible, in telling in one play the significant aspects of the history of civilization. I take particular delight in *The Skin of Our Teeth* because it seems to illustrate and prove, within a single drama, my thesis that theatre can be educationally vital, and because, at its best, it teaches all the lessons of history, all the problems of society, and all the beauty in nature, in the very palatable form of entertainment. It is important that students be told that, in spite of its broad scope and serious theme, this play is highly entertaining and very amusing. Encourage them to relax and enjoy it!

Glossary of Allusions in the Play

ADAM AND EVE: According to the first book of the *Bible*, Genesis, Adam was the first man and Eve the first woman, and they were to "have dominion over the fish of the sea, and over the fowl of the air, and over every living thing that moveth upon the earth."

GENESIS II:18:   This reference is also to the *Bible* and is used in the play as a symbol of the beginning of the Antrobus family and hence the human family. This verse reads: "And the Lord God said, 'It is not good that man should be alone; I will make him an help mate for him.'"

ANTROBUS: This is the family name given to the leading characters in the play because they represent all mankind in every country and age. Mr. and Mrs. Antrobus are Adam and Eve, Mr. and Mrs. Human, Mr. and Mrs. Everyman, and John and Jane Doe.

PEG O' MY HEART, SMILIN' THRU, THE BAT, RAIN, THE BARRETTS OF WIMPOLE STREET, FIRST LADY: Popular plays of the period from 1915 through 1935, in which the actors who appear in *The Skin of Our Teeth* have performed during previous Broadway seasons.

MAMMOTH: A Stone Age animal somewhat similar to an elephant.

DINOSAUR: A prehistoric animal. In this play both of these animals are household pets of the Antrobus family, somewhat like the dogs and cats modern families own.

ICE AGE: The period, probably a million years ago, during which the entire earth's surface was covered with glaciers. It is used in the play as a symbol of one of the apparently insurmountable catastrophes that human and animal life on the earth has managed to survive—"by the skin of our teeth."

CAIN AND ABEL: They are the two sons of Adam and Eve. According to the *Bible*, Cain was a farmer and Abel a keeper of sheep. Cain became angry and killed his brother Abel. Cain, a fugitive and a vagabond upon the earth, had put a mark upon his forehead so that anyone who found him could identify him as a murderer. Cain has therefore become a symbol of evil. In the play, Henry Antrobus represents Cain, and, therefore the evil in the world. Henry also has the "Mark of Cain"—an ugly red scar shaped like the letter "C"—on his forehead.

MUSES: In Greek mythology, the Muses are the nine daughters of Jupiter who are the patron goddesses of the arts and sciences. In the play, they are among the refugees whom Mr. Antrobus takes into his home so that they may escape the approaching glaciers and survive the Ice Age.

JUDGE MOSES: In the Old Testament of the *Bible*, Moses is the heroic and wise leader who delivers the Jews from slavery in Egypt and leads them to their Promised Land. In the play, he is also a refugee from the glaciers.

THE TEN COMMANDMENTS: The fundamental laws of the Jewish (and later the Christian) religion, which God gave to Moses to be used as standards of behavior for his people. They are found in Exodus XX:1-17.

HOMER: A Greek poet who is believed to have written *The Iliad* and *The Odyssey* and who was blind. In the play, he is another of the refugees whom Mr. Antrobus shelters from the glaciers.

HELEN OF TROY: The beautiful wife of Paris, who was the cause of the war that caused the destruction of Troy.

ORDER OF MAMMALS: Scientific name for man and other animals who nurse their young. In the play, they constitute a fraternal organization and have elected Mr. Antrobus their new president at an international conventon.

THE WINGS, THE FINS, AND THE SHELLS: Other kinds of animals (birds, fish, and mollusks, who send delegates to to the convention.

THE BOARDWALK: A sidewalk built along the beach at Atlantic City, New Jersey. It is a noted resort and amusement center, and it is the location of the convention.

PLAGUES: Any disease that becomes so widespread as to be out of control. Before the development of modern medicine, there were many such plagues, which nearly wiped out entire cities.

VIVIPAROUS, HAIRY, AND DIAPHRAGMATIC: Animals that carry their young within the body, have hair, and breathe with lungs rather than gills. These are characteristics common to all mammals and used by Mr. Antrobus to prove his complete loyalty and conformity to the Order in a campaign speech for the presidency.

CRUSADE FOR MARRIAGE: Mrs. Antrobus, in a speech for the Ladies' Auxiliary of the Ancient and Honorable Order of Mammals, refers to the successful efforts of women to formalize marriage into a church and civil ceremony and a legal contract rather than to continue the "common law" marriage—by consent of both parties.

BRIGHT'S DISEASE: A kidney disease, which may be fatal.

CIRRHOSIS OF THE LIVER: A disease characterized by the formation of abnormal tissue in the liver.

APOPLEXY: A heart or circulatory illness, which is caused by an obstruction in the artery of the brain.

CHARLATAN: A quack, phony, or pretender to knowledge and ability in any field.

"I AM A SULTAN, LET MY SLAVE-GIRLS FAN ME":   This quotation from the Fortune Teller's speech refers to man's laziness and his attitude that he need not work because the world owes him a living.

THE FLOOD: The great flood referred to in the *Bible* when Noah took his family and two animals (one male and one female) of each kind into the ark. They were the only survivors of the flood.

THE DELUGE: The forty days and forty nights of rain, which the *Bible* tells caused the Great Flood.

NOAH'S ARK: The ship built by Noah to save his family and the animals from the flood. In the play, the ship on which Mr. Antrobus loads the animals and his family is a symbol of Noah's Ark.

JEREMIAH: A prophet of the Old Testament, often referred to as the prophet of doom because of his pessimism. In the play, the people call the Fortune Teller Jeremiah because she is warning them of their doom.

PHI BETA KAPPA: A scholastic honor conferred upon outstanding university students.

EQUITY: The name of the union of stage actors.

SABINA: The servant of the Antrobus family, who represents the "other woman" trying to break up the home.

ARISTOTLE: A Greek philosopher who is considered to be one of the great thinkers of all time.

PLATO: A Greek philosopher who was a student of Socrates and teacher of Aristotle. His *Republic* is often referred to by modern political scientists.

SPINOZA: A noted Dutch philosopher.

WHEEL, LEVER, ALPHABET: These are major inventions of man upon which the progress of civilization has been built. In the play, Mr. Antrobus, because he is universal man, is the inventor of all these things.

The Glass Menagerie seemed to require a different sort of audience preparation than most other plays, and a bulletin was prepared, which attempted to clarify the interpretation and meaning of this play.

The Glass Menagerie is a particularly moving play about the relationships between a mother, her son, and her daughter. Amanda, the mother whose husband has deserted the family, is anxious to have her children succeed. The daughter, Laura, is slightly crippled and has become so shy that she cannot face people outside the family. The son, Tom, works in a factory to support his mother and sister, but dreams of finding adventure as a merchant seaman and writer.

The Glass Menagerie is unconventional in its setting and plot structure. The author calls it poetic realism because it contains only that which is essential to present a clear portrait of the important characteristics of each of the members of the family.

The reasons for selection of this play are many, but the overriding factor is that its subject matter may help the student audience find an insight into themselves and their own families, that they might not otherwise acquire except through the perspective of many years.

In this production we are trying to focus attention upon the mother's attempts to help her children find themselves and assume the responsibilities of adults. What Amanda Wingfield's children cannot see, but we hope our audience will understand, is that she is not merely a nagging mother; Amanda is a rather pitiful, heroic woman trying vainly to give her children "courage for living." In this sense, Amanda is all mothers when she says, "I'll tell you what I wished for on the moon. Success and happiness for my precious children. I wish for that whenever there's a moon, and when there isn't a moon, I wish for it, too."

The tragedy for Amanda is not the loss of her own comfort and gracious Southern way of life, but her failure to make her wishes for her children come true.

In presenting this play in an atmosphere in which we concentrate upon understanding children, perhaps we are asking, in a small voice, for a brief moment in which the children attempt to understand parents.

It must be apparent by now that these bulletins are designed to acquaint faculty members with the values of drama in education, as well as to prepare students for their experiences as members of an audience. Most teachers are pleased to learn of the important role that drama can play in education and of the assistance it can offer them in their own classrooms. Because personnel on any faculty gradually changes, it is useful for the drama teacher, periodically, to restate the reasons for producing plays for a high school audience. The following bulletin, issued before the presentation of a play that required relatively little audience preparation, is an example of a restatement of purpose.

> As you may know, the members of our Play Production Class will present Thornton Wilder's new play, *The Matchmaker,* in an extended assembly period. Perhaps you may be interested in the reasons for the inclusion of play productions in the curriculum, and in some discussion of the material in this particular play.
>
> *Point of View:* In the past decade, there has been an exciting revolution in the play production program in the high school. Theater in the high school has moved from the school's recreational activities into its educational program. Like music, literature, and art, drama in the high school is *not vocational education;* it is designed to provide general education in the broad area of the humanities. The production of the play is intended primarily to enhance the cultural background of the entire student body, by introducing them to plays with literary merit as well as entertainment value. In a democratic society, cultural experience should not be the private prerogative of an elite class who can afford to be "patrons of the arts." It is therefore both the privilege and the obligation of the drama department in a public school to offer opportunities for cultural education to all students. It is in this context that we seek to present those important ideas and ideals that are most easily understood in their dramatic forms— the lessons of history, the problems of society, and the beautiful in human nature. It is also this philosophy of audience education that has dictated the selection, in recent years, of such productions as *Family Portrait, The Importance of Being Earnest, You Can't Take It With You, Dear Brutus, Our Town, The Crucible, The Skin of Our Teeth, The Cradle Song, Medea,* and *The Glass Menagerie.*
>
> *Information on The Matchmaker:* (The following material may be useful to you in discussing this play with your classes.)
>
> *The Matchmaker,* a rewritten version of *The Merchant of Yonkers,* which Thornton Wilder wrote in 1938, is based upon Johann Nestroy's *Einen Jux will es sich Machen* (1842), which was based upon John Oxenford's *A Day Well Spent* (1835). That *The Matchmaker* is the third of Mr. Wilder's plays to be presented here in the past four years may be only an indication of the theatrical tastes of the director, but it is probably also a comment upon Wilder's importance among contemporary American playwrights. At any rate, Thornton Wilder (who was a teacher himself) offers much in his

plays that a teacher can recommend to his students. In *The Matchmaker,* as in his other plays, Mr. Wilder observes man with his weaknesses, his follies, and his virtues, and concludes that he is mostly good, highly amusing, and worthy of being entrusted with the future.

Because *The Matchmaker* is a fast-moving and highly entertaining farce, there is some danger that the play's theme may be drowned out in laughter. To prevent this, the author has several characters step out of the picture frame and explain their thoughts to the audience. Some excerpts from these soliloquies will illustrate the theme.

"Yes, like all you other fools, I'm willing to risk a little security for a certain amount of adventure. Think it over."

"I'm in danger of losing my job and my future and everything that people think is important; but I don't care. Even if I have to dig ditches the rest of my life, I'll be a ditch-digger who once had a wonderful day."

"But there comes a moment in everybody's life when he must decide whether he'll live among human beings or not—a fool among fools or a fool alone. . . . And suddenly I realized that for a long time I had not shed one tear; nor had I been for one moment outrageously happy; nor had I been filled with wonderful hope that something or other would turn out well. . . . I decided to rejoin the human race. . . . If you accept human beings and are willing to live among them, you acknowledge that every man has a right to his own mistakes."

"I think it's about adventure. The test of an adventure is that when you're in the middle of it, you say to yourself; 'Oh, now I've got myself into an awful mess; I wish I were sitting quietly at home'. . . . We all hope that in your lives you have just the right amount of sitting quietly at home and just the right amount of adventure."

A more concise statement of theme might be: "But who can know, as the long years go, that to live is happy has found his paradise!" or "In the time of your life—live!"

Mr. Wilder presents his theme through a story of a wealthy widower who hires a "matchmaker" to find him a suitable wife. After four acts of hilarious antics, the widower, his two employees, his niece, and his friends settle down to lives in which there is "just the right amount of adventure and just the right amount of sitting quietly at home."

Another approach to the preparation of the student audience through English classes is illustrated by the following memo:

To: English Teachers

Re: *Hamlet* as lesson in English Classes.

The following is an attempt to answer the requests I have had from a *few* teachers for assistance in relating this week's production of *Hamlet* to the class work in English. It is experimental. I do not know whether it will prove helpful. You are *not required* to make use of the ideas and suggestions herein. All of this may prove worthless, but I've been promising myself for twelve years that I'd try this project, and I'm going to have a go at it. O.K.?

LESSON PLAN (OR SOMETHING) *Objective:* To help students overcome dislike of Shakespeare, by making them realize that they are smart enough to understand his writing.

Method: Discussion and analysis of a segment of *Hamlet*.

Techniques:
1. Leading questions.
2. Teacher "translation."
3. Student comment.
4. Relation of ideas and emotions to personal experiences and students.

Materials:
1. The "To be or not to be" soliloquy.
2. Plot information.

The Plan:
1. Read simple plot summary of *Hamlet* to class.
2. Read preliminary situation to soliloquy to class.
3. Read soliloquy to class.
4. Interpret, understand soliloquy through question and answers, paraphrasing, and discussion.

PLOT SUMMARY: *Hamlet* tells the story of a Prince of Denmark who learns that his father has been murdered and attempts to avenge that murder. Hamlet discovers that his father was killed by Claudius, who has married the widowed queen Gertrude and thereby usurped the throne of Denmark. Hamlet's revenge proves futile, because it brings about his own death and that of his mother (Gertrude), his sweetheart (Ophelia), and Ophelia's father (Polonius) and brother (Laertes), along with the death of the evil Claudius.

SITUATION PRIOR TO SOLILOQUY: Hamlet has become convinced that his father was murdered by Claudius. He is struggling with his own conscience to decide what he should do about the murder.

SOLILOQUY:

I

To be, or not to be, that is the question—Whether 'tis nobler in the mind to suffer the slings and arrows of outrageous fortune, or to take arms against a sea of troubles, and by opposing, end them.

II   To Die, to sleep—

No more;

III

and by that sleep to say we end the heartache and the thousand natural shocks that flesh is heir to; 'tis a consummation devoutly to be wished.

IV   To die, to sleep—

to sleep, perchance to dream,

V

aye, there's the rub, for in that sleep of death what dreams may come when we have shuffled off this mortal coil, must give us pause;

VI

There's the respect that makes calamity of so long life.

VII

For who would bear the whips and scorns of time, the oppressor's wrong, the proud man's contumely, the pangs of despised love, the law's delay, the insolence of office, and the spurns that patient merit of the unworthy takes, when he himself might his quietus make with a bare bodkin?

VIII

Who would fardels bear, to grunt and sweat under a weary life,

IX

But that the dread of something after death,

X

The undiscovered country, from whose bourn no traveler returns, puzzles the will,

XI

And makes us rather bear those ills we have, than fly to others that we know not of?

XII

Thus conscience does make cowards of us all,

XIII

And thus the native hue of resolution is sicklied o'er with the pale cast of thought,

XIV

And enterprises of great pitch and moment with this regard their currents turn awry, and lose the name of action.

NOTE: The soliloquy is broken into phrases, which make up units of a single idea or emotion. There are transitions, indicated by the spaces between these sections.

If you practice reading this aloud and practice reading it with emotion and characterization as well as intellect, it should make an effective device for teaching.

After the first reading, try reading it by sections and asking such questions as:

1. What did he say in those lines?

2. Why did he use that word?

3. How does he feel?

4. Why does he worry so much?

5. Have you ever thought about death and what may come after it?

Program Notes

The program printed for each high school play can make a valuable contribution to the relationship between the audience and the production. First, by its design, color, and content, the program should tell the audience what kind of play they are to see. It should set the mood of 'the play so that the audience will know how it is expected to behave and to react. More important, the program should give information about the playwright, the ideas, the characters, the situation, and the theme of the play so that the audience may more fully appreciate what they see. The program will serve to prepare those students who have not been members of a class that studied the play in advance, as well as to enhance the enjoyment of parents and others who see the play. As in the case of classroom materials, the nature and extent of program notes must depend upon the particular play being presented. Here are some examples.

These notes, from the program of *Medea* give the historical background of the play.

> The first written drama of Western civilization developed in Greece in about the sixth century B.C., and was designed to be both a tribute to gods and a means of teaching the Greek people the legend, philosophy, and ethics of their progenitors. In the relatively brief span of two centuries, Greece produced four playwrights (Aeschylus, Sophocles, Euripides, and Aristophanes) whose works were of such magnitude as to cause them to become the cornerstones of western theatre and to be still produced after three thousand years.

> Euripides' *Medea* ranks as one of the great plays of all time, and the translation of it being presented here is the adaptation which the noted California poet, Robinson Jeffers, wrote for Judith Anderson in 1946. Miss Anderson played the title role on Broadway and on tour for two years. Its popularity with modern American audiences proved once more that an emotionally powerful play that encompasses universal ideas and characters may be appreciated and understood, in spite of the barriers of thousands of miles of space and three thousand years of time. Pre-Christian Greece and twentieth century America, as well as all the nations and ages between these two, are able to sympathize with a deserted wife, be concerned about the custody of her children, and understand her desire for revenge.

> *Medea*, like most Greek plays, is based upon one of the legends, *The Golden Fleece*. Before the action of the play begins, Jason, whose kingdom in Greece has been usurped, makes a voyage to Asiatic Colchis to obtain the sacred Golden Fleece and thereby prove himself worthy to regain his position. Medea, the daughter of the ruler of Colchis, falls in love with Jason, turns against her family to help him steal the Golden Fleece, and flees with him to his home in Greece. Several years later Jason, hoping to gain more power, abandons Medea and their two sons to marry the daughter of Creon, ruler of Corinth. The play's story begins shortly after Jason's

new marriage, as Medea seeks the violent revenge that she believes will punish Jason and make her own grief more bearable.

For the production of *Rhinoceros,* an explanation of the Absurdists' style and purpose seemed appropriate.

Eugene Ionesco was the first of the school of Absurd playwrights to emerge in France in the Fifties. He is one of the most popular of the avant-garde, because he, unlike many others of the Absurdists, is able to express his themes clearly in spite of the façade of nonsense that covers them.

Although his earliest plays were rejected by critics, his work is now widely acclaimed. "The Lesson," presented in Paris on February 20, 1951, was his first critical success in France. A production of "The Chairs" at the Phoenix Theatre in New York on January 9, 1958, brought Ionesco's work to America, where Broadway critics praised his unique style.

In his introduction to an English translation of the two plays mentioned above, William Saroyan says, "He seems to find the world entirely laughable. His plays . . . bewilder, delight, annoy, astonish, amaze, and amuse me. . . . Who told him to transform lunacy into a thing of greater beauty than mathematics itself? What triggered this Romanian in Paris, at the age of forty-five? Ionesco most likely would prefer people to laugh. Laugh all you like, but just try to forget what you saw and how it made you feel. You can't, it was art. It was new art."

Famed British drama critic Kenneth Tynan calls Ionesco "a poet of double talk." He points out that Ionesco's plays are built in two stories, "farcical at street level . . . tragic one flight up." *Rhinoceros* is an excellent example of Ionesco's skill on both the farcical and tragic levels. What could be more absurdly funny than the citizens of a village turning into a herd of rhinoceroses, as they do in the simple plot of this play? What could be more tragic than the total inability of these people to maintain sufficient individuality to resist conforming to the herd—even the ridiculous herd of rhinoceros?

What sets Ionesco above his Absurdist colleagues of the theatre is his ability to make the elaborate symbols of this literary style work. Everyone who sees *Rhinoceros* will know that the conflict is between logic and fashion, between individuality and conformity. Whether the symbolic rhinoceros herd represents mini-skirts or Neo-Nazism, the symbol is clear to all. The nonsense makes sense!

The program notes for *Hamlet* were designed to help students understand Shakespeare's greatness.

Hamlet and *Julius Caesar,* both written by Shakespeare in 1600 when he was thirty-six years of age, began his "tragic period" as a playwright, during which his greatest plays were written. More than 350 years after its birth, *Hamlet* retains its youth on the living stage and is generally considered to be the greatest drama of all time. Its continuing appeal to audiences lies not in its recording of an incident in the history of Denmark, but rather in the universality of the characters and the beauty of the language.

Hamlet, the noble Prince who must put aside his mourning over the death of his father in order to avenge his father's murder, has provided a challenge to every great actor since Shakespeare's time. The tragedy of Hamlet's fate has been understood and pitied by audiences of all kinds. As the audiences admire Hamlet, they pity Ophelia, laugh with the grave-diggers, hate the crafty, evil Claudius, and regard Polonius with kindly amused tolerance.

Almost daily, quotations from HAMLET are heard in ordinary conversations. Often the source of these expressions is unknown to those who say, "Something is rotten in Denmark"; "Neither a borrower nor a lender be"; "Sweets to the sweet"; "This is above all, to thine own self be true"; "Aye, there's the rub"; "To be or not to be"; "Frailty, thy name is woman"? "One may smile and smile and be a villain"; "Brevity is the soul of wit"; "Good night, sweet prince."

The universality of the characters and the many memorable lines were what caused Ben Jonson to write of Shakespeare, "He was not of an age but of all time."

Hamlet has been selected for presentation at Canoga Park High School not because of the quadricentennial of Shakespeare's birth, but rather for two more important reasons. First, the present high quality of student talent among actors, designers, technicians, and crew members suggested that they could do justice to this most challenging of all plays from the pen of the greatest of all playwrights. Second, the obligation of the high school to give its students the best possible material in drama, just as it does in literature, math, music, science, and art, demanded that *Hamlet* be produced.

One of the noted contemporary philosophers, Alfred North Whitehead, urged that "education must involve an exposure to greatness." Jerome S. Bruner underscores this idea by stating that "The nurturing of images of excellence is the principle function of the schools."

In an effort to involve the participants in the greatness of Shakespeare's genius and to expose the student audience to his image of excellence, Canoga Park High School presents *Hamlet*.

Special Productions for Subject Disciplines

On occasion, the drama teacher may wish to prepare a special season or series of plays or concert readings for a particular audience. Although it isn't possible to stage all plays that appear in required English textbooks, it may be possible to have drama students prepare concert readings of some of these plays and present them to an invited audience of classes who are studying them. *Our Town* is read so universally in American literature classes that it can be read for those classes each semester.

The social studies curriculum offers the drama teacher countless opportunities to select plays that relate directly to events and ideas being studied in classes. For seniors studying the U.S. Government at Canoga Park High School a few years ago, the advanced drama classes presented a series of productions under the title "We Hold These Truths." The series consisted of concert readings of *An Enemy of the People,* which deals with the obligations of citizenship in a democracy; *Harriet,* a biography of Harriet Beecher Stowe with passages from *Uncle Tom's Cabin: The Devil's Disciple,* a witty commentary on Colonial America: *A Raisin in the Sun,* a comedy-drama about racial segregation; and a fully produced presentation of *The Male Animal,* a comedy which deals with the serious problem of academic freedom. Together, these plays probably did more to create for the students an understanding of the principles which underlie the American system of government than did the textbook they were studying concurrently.

A strong emphasis upon education of the high school student audience can serve to broaden the scope and improve the status of drama in the school. For the teacher-director, focus upon audience education offers an opportunity to prove that theatre is the most universal of all the arts, the most human of all the humanities, and the most helpful of all the audio-visual aids.

TEACHING DRAMA CLASSES AND DIRECTING PLAYS FOR HIGH SCHOOL

PART III

CHAPTER 9

Planning a Beginning Drama Course of Study

The introductory course in drama at the high school level is the most difficult one to plan and to teach, because it must serve both general educational goals and specialized subject matter objectives for students with widely divergent interests and abilities. Any student in the high school should be permitted, in fact encouraged, to enroll in a beginning drama class. The course should enhance the general cultural background and develop an appreciation of the art of the theatre for every student who enrolls in it. The student with special interest and ability in theatre will also need this general background, along with beginning techniques of theatrical performance. For the high school drama teacher-director, the beginning course is the foundation upon which he must build his entire drama program. He must discover the potentially talented students, begin their disciplined training in the arts and crafts of theatre, and encourage them to continue their development in more advanced courses.

Perhaps the most difficult problems in teaching a beginning drama course arise from the attitudes that students bring with them. Some are there because a parent or counselor thought drama would be good for them. Some enroll because they have a heavy academic load and want an easy course. Some are star-struck and feel they are destined to replace Rock Hudson. Some couldn't get into any other class period three! Few, if any, expect to read, write, study, and prepare homework as they would in other courses. At the outset, the teacher should describe the nature of the course to his class and explain that success in the drama class will require as much time and study as most other classes. He should explain that the beginning drama class is not primarily an acting class; it is an introduction to theatre combined with an introduction to acting. It is as much work as other classes, but for most students, it is also more fun than other studies.

Content of Beginning Course

To serve both the general educational and the prevocational needs of students, the beginning drama course should include the following units' of study:

> dramatic literature;
> theatre history;
> evaluation of performance;
> pantomime and movement;
> voice, diction, and oral interpretation;
> classroom scenes.

Since each of the units suggested would constitute at least one complete and separate course in a college, it is obvious that budgeting time is an important aspect of teaching a beginning drama class and that the teacher must be highly selective in deciding what to include in each area of study. The problem is to put infinity into an eighteen weeks span of time in a twenty-five by forty classroom. In the class time available, approximately two weeks can be spent on dramatic literature, three on theatre history, three on pantomime and movement, two on voice, diction, and oral interpretation, and eight on classroom scenes. The evaluation of theatrical performances is interwoven with the other units as the occasions arise.

Who Has Talent?

Before detailing the specific content of each area to be studied in a beginning drama class, it might be valuable to discuss means by which the teacher can discover which students are potentially talented. To be sure, some of the talented students will demonstrate their creativity by the quality of their early assignments in pantomime, but often the most talented students will be too self-critical to perform well. Sometimes they will claim to be unprepared and refuse to perform at all, rather than risk the humiliation of performing poorly. Is that student in the third row who always says, "I didn't prepare it," lazy or a highly sensitive perfectionist? The drama teacher should try to discover which he is.

Almost nothing is known about the nature of theatrical talent. There are no standardized tests that will select the creative students, much less those whose creativity can be best expressed in the theatre arts. Our knowledge and recognition of the theatrically talented student is based upon, and limited by, our personal observations and experiences. Accordingly, the following unscientific observations are offered about the characteristics of the talented drama student. He has above average intelligence; however, his academic achievement may range from very poor to outstandingly good. (This does not mean that all students with high I.Q.'s are talented. There seems to be no relationship between I.Q. and talent, except that the talented student is never of low intelligence. He is highly critical of himself and of others. He is often very quiet and shy. He is highly observant of his physical environment and of human behavior. He is emotionally sensitive, and therefore easily hurt or discouraged.

Because some important characteristics of the talented student cannot be readily observed by the drama teacher. Two game-like observation tests may be given to students early in the semester. In administering both of the following tests, it is important that the students not be given details of their purposes.

Test I—Observation of Inanimate Objects

The teacher brings half a dozen objects to class, such as an old shoe, a scrap of velvet, a sea shell, an empty cigar box, an onion, a fresh flower, a bag of gum drops. All objects are passed around the class, and students are asked to examine them carefully. They may eat a gum drop if they wish. When each object has been around the class, it should be placed at the front of the room. Students are then asked to write a description of each article, giving as much detail as possible. They are told that they may reexamine the articles if they wish and are encouraged to spend the entire class period writing.

Evaluation of Test:

The purpose of this test is to check each student's degree of sensory perception and creative projection. In evaluating the papers, the teacher can count how many times each of the five senses is used to describe each object. In addition to describing the objects, some students will mention personal experiences related to these objects or will describe people who might have owned or used them.

Test II—Observation of Human Behavior

Select two members of the class who are known to be close friends. Without informing the rest of the class, ask these two students to stage a brief scene in class, in which they appear to have a serious quarrel. Perhaps they may exchange notes and angry glances. One may ask to leave the class. A few moments later, the other may run out of the classroom without permission. When both have left, ask the class to write a paper describing the behavior of the two friends. Encourage the students to use the rest of the class period for the assignment. Give them no suggestions, except that they include as much detail as they can.

EVALUATION OF TEST:

The purpose of this test is to learn how aware students are of those around them. Check the papers first for accuracy in describing the details of the incident and then for projection of those actions into an explanation of the situation and the motives of each of the characters.

Because observation and imagination are essential attributes of the creative artist, these two tests may help the drama teacher to decide which students are potentially talented. They may guide the teacher in encouraging some sudents who might not develop or reveal their potential on their own initiative. If these students are encouraged, their achievements on the subsequent performing assignments will reveal whether their creativity should be channeled into theatre or one of the other arts.

Dramatic Literature

The raw material of all the arts of the theatre is the play script. The beginning drama student therefore must first learn to read and understand the play script and must next acquire as extensive a background in dramatic literature of all nations and times as is possible. Techniques of play reading, as well as an outline for play analysis, are discussed in detail in Chapter 15. The student should begin his study of plays by reading an explanation of the structure, styles, and types of drama in a standard textbook. Katharine Anne Ommaney's *The Stage and The School* [1] is excellent for this purpose, and has been the standard textbook for beginning high school drama for over thirty-five years. There are few competing texts, and none is as comprehensive as Ommaney's. During the beginning course, each student should read and write analyses of six or seven plays by major playwrights. To help students learn how to read and analyze a play, one may be selected to be read in class and analyzed with the help of the teacher. Students should then be able to read and analyze plays independently, with the teacher evaluating and commenting on each student report. So that students will enjoy and benefit from these reading assignments, it may be wise to require that they select the plays from a list similar to the one found in Appendix A. They

[1] Katharine A. Ommaney, *The Stage and the School,* 3rd ed. (New York: McGraw-Hill Book Company, 1960).

should be encouraged to read plays of different playwrights, periods, and countries. Student interest in the plays may be stimulated by the teacher's discussing the characteristics of some of the playwrights and plays on the list. Certainly, no student should emerge from a drama class without knowing something about Shakespeare, Goldsmith, Sheridan, Moliere, Ibsen, Shaw, O'Neill, Williams, Miller, and Wilder.

In addition to gaining background in dramatice literature through these assignments, students will be building up a knowledge of plays from which they can select scenes for acting assignments later in the course.

Theatre History

A knowledge and an understanding of the history and evolution of the theatre in Western civilization is valuable to the student in a beginning drama class in many ways. Obviously, it will help him understand the plays from various eras and the manner in which they were originally produced. In studying the theatre of each period, he will acquire an understanding of the society that spawned it, for drama deals with the impact of events and environment upon man. The study of theatre history may help the student see the relationships among the various segments of history he has studied in other courses.

The Stage and the School [2] contains a concise section on theatre history, which can be used to supplement classroom lectures. In order to make theatre history meaningful, the teacher should relate the developments in theatre to the history and culture of each period. To clarify the social setting and to motivate student interest, the teacher may tell the stories of one or two famous plays from each era.

A useful device for helping students learn theatre history is an outline chart like the one started on the next page. Students can put the headings for these columns in their notebooks and fill in the columns as each historical period is discussed in class. When the chart is completed, it will provide a quick review of the highlights of each period and an outline of the chronology of every aspect of theatre.

The discussion of each period should begin with the last column on the chart, Contemporary Names and Events. The information for this column should be drawn from the students by questions like these: Have you ever heard of the Golden Age of Greece? Why was it called that? If a man from the Golden Age walked in this room, would you know where he came from? What would he be wearing? Who were some of the famous Greeks? Students will respond with names and events like those entered on the chart. This approach to theatre history has two advantages. It offers the students an opportunity to recall, with pride,

2 Ommaney, *op. cit.*

Period	Place	Dates	Physical Theatre	Playwrights	Plays	Others in Theatre	Contemporary Names and Events
Golden Age of Greece	Athens	6th-4th Centuries B.C.	Outdoor, hillside for audience, stage at foot of hill.	Aeschylus Sophocles Euripides Aristophanes	Oresteia Oedipus Rex Medea The Frogs	Aristotle (critic) Thespis (actor)	The Old Testament Homer (9th Century B.C.) Socrates, Plato, Aristotle, Euclid, Pythagoras, Hippocrates Peloponnesian War
Roman	Rome	3rd Century B.C. 3rd Century A.D.					Birth of Christ The New Testament
Dark Ages	Europe	4th-10th Centuries A.D.					Feudalism
Medieval	Europe	9th-15th Centuries A.D.					The Crusaders— 1096-1270 A.D. Discovery of America
Renaissance	Italy & Europe	14th-16th Centuries A.D.					
Elizabethan	England	Late 16th-Early 17th Centuries					Puritan New England
Restoration	England France	1660-1700					
18th Century	England & Europe	1700-1800					American Revolution
19th Century	England Europe America	1800-1900					1860-Industrial revolution-urban, democratic society
Modern	Europe England America	1890-Present					

what they already know about the period being studied, and it gives them a background of familiar names and events with which to associate the theatre history. If students fail to offer some of the more significant names and events, the teacher should, of course, add them.

Teachers should perhaps be warned against requiring students to learn more than they want to know, or need to know, about theatre history. They should know enough about the physical theatre of each period to understand how it affected the staging of plays, but they need not know enough to reconstruct the theatre. Students should know the major playwrights and great plays of each period. Sophocles, Shakespeare, Ibsen, Shaw, and Wilder are important to beginning students, but they need not know Beaumont and Fletcher, Wycherley, Galsworthy, and Fitch.

The beginning drama student should learn enough about theatre history to make him aware of the evolutionary development of theatre so that he may see how modern theatre has been influenced by theatres of the past. He may also begin to recognize some of the universalities of human ideas, experiences, and emotions, which are reflected in the theatre of every period.

Evaluation of Performances

No aspect of the beginning drama class is more important both to the student's general background and to his personal progress as a performer than learning to analyze and evaluate theatrical performances. During the semester, the student should have guided experience in criticizing two levels of performances: (1) presentations of plays in the theatre or on television, and (2) classroom presentations of acting exercises by his fellow students.

During the semester, each student should be required to write critiques of two plays seen in a theatre and of three plays seen on television. These five assignments, together with the six or seven analyses of plays read, should provide beginning drama students with a valuable introduction to dramatic literature and criticism. The assignments also constitute a substantial amount of writing for every student, which may pacify those who are concerned about the academic respectability of drama classes!

As was suggested in introducing students to play reading, a common viewing experience is probably the best way to introduce students to the process of evaluating theatrical performances. All students may be assigned to see the same television play. Professional reviews of it may be brought into class and read by all. Students and teacher may then hold a discussion of the performance based on both the students' reactions and opinions and those of the professional critics. It is important to point out which aspects of the production—script, acting, setting, and so on—

the critics comment upon, so that they may use this information in writing their subsequent individual reviews.

To expose students to some of the better dramatic material offered on television, the teacher may require them to write their reviews only on recommended shows. The following qualifications serve to define what television plays are acceptable for this assignment.

> They must be at least one hour long.
>
> They must have been produced for television, not for motion pictures.
>
> They must be individual dramas, not one of a series with continuing characters or a continuing story.

It may be convenient to provide students with an outline, like the following, for their television reviews.

    I. Identification of program
        A. Title of program
        B. Title of play
        C. Date, time, and station
        D. Personnel
            1. Author
            2. Director
            3. Producer
            4. Major actors
   II. Plot summary (200 word maximum)
  III. Dramatic analysis
        A. Type
        B. Style
        C. Kind of conflict
        D. Protagonist
        E. Antagonist
        F. Theme
   IV. Essay of evaluation
        (Discuss your opinion of all the aspects of this production. Be sure to tell why you reacted as you did to it.)

As mentioned in Chapter 14, where a sample student review of a play seen in a theatre is also given, students are asked to write play reviews as if they were newspaper critics. They are given no specific outline, but are encouraged to read professional drama critics in order to observe their techniques of criticsm.

Student evaluation of classroom acting exercises can be valuable to both the critics and the performers if it is properly handled. The first critiques of classroom performances should be given by the teacher so that students who give later critiques may follow his example. The critic should begin by pointing out any positive values the performance may have. Next, he should mention the weakness of the performances and offer suggestions about how the performance might be improved. The criticism must never become personal. The characterization and interpretation should be criticized, never the actor himself. Student critics who become rude to their classmates should be reprimanded rather severely. In order to save class time, as well as to avoid a situation in which the entire class criticizes one student, it is wise to appoint one critic to evaluate each performance and to give that critic a set of criteria upon which to base his comments. Each critique by a student should be followed by comments from the teacher, which take note of the student critique and supplement it.

Pantomime and Movement

No topic evokes more controversy among drama teachers than the teaching of acting. The author of this text believes that the introductory instruction in acting, which is included in the beginning drama class, should be divided into the general areas of pantomime and movement, voice, diction, and oral interpretation, and classroom scenes. This approach to the problem, like the other suggestions in this text, is based upon personal experience. It has worked for this author. It may work for others.

Perhaps some additional comments about the nature of acting and its teaching may be helpful in understanding these beginning acting assignments. Although talent is an important element in the theatre, few professional companies, much less high school groups, are comprised entirely of talented actors. Many good performances are turned in by competent, well-trained actors, who have relatively little talent. Any normally intelligent individual who applies himself to the task can learn to act, just as any normally intelligent individual who applies himself to the task can learn to play a musical instrument. How well he learns to act or to play an instrument will depend upon the degree of talent he has. At the beginning level, acting, like music, is based upon mastering certain elementary techniques. These techniques should be included in the beginning high school drama class.

Pantomime is the best activity with which to begin teaching acting, because it isolates the area of characterization of which most people are least aware. Acting is physical, verbal, and emotional. With the verbal aspect withdrawn, students can be made aware of the importance of the physical as a reflection and expression of the emotional. In preparation for their assignments in pantomime, students may be asked to observe a stranger and to write a detailed description of him. They should include not only the physical aspects of the stranger but also their guesses about the emotional qualities of their subject. These descriptions may be read aloud in class, with attention directed to how much we may learn about a person by observing his clothing, posture, gestures, walk, and facial expression.

With this background, the students are asked to create a written description of an imaginary character whom they will portray for the class by walking across the stage. It should be suggested that they create characters different from themselves in age and personality. Through class discussion, the students may prepare an outline to guide them in describing their imaginary characters. As was suggested for the history chart, those important elements of character description that the students fail to include should be added by the teacher. Presented with the question—"What will you need to know about your imaginary character in order to portray him walking across the stage?"—students will develop an outline something like the following:

> Outline for Imaginary Character
> I. Physical
>   A. Age
>   B. Sex
>   C. Hair—color and style
>   D. Clothing and grooming—detailed
>   E. Posture
>   F. Mannerisms
>   G. Condition of health
>   H. Weight, height, build
> II. Emotional—Internal Makeup
>   A. General disposition
>   B. Attitude toward life and people
>   C. Interests and occupation
>   D. Present mood
> III. External Environment
>   A. Location
>   B. Weather conditions
>   C. Surface on which he is walking
>   D. Destination
>   1. Where is he going?
>   2. Why?

Many students will feel, and a few may express, a fear of their ability to create an imaginary character. These students should be reassured by being told that there is no such thing as abstract imagination. Rather, what we call imagination is the process of putting together our observations and experiences in unique combinations. After the students have created their imaginary characters on paper, they should practice portraying them. In their imaginations, they should try on the clothing, body, and personality of their character and practice walking around in them. After each student has portrayed his character by walking across the stage, the members of the class may be asked to describe who and what they saw. The teacher should then read the outline to determine whether the student actor has communicated what he intended to the audience. If he has not, the reason for his failure usually lies in insufficient knowledge of the character, which will be revealed by an inadequate character description. Occasionally the failure will lie in insufficient rehearsal or in self-consciousness on the part of the beginner. Both of these faults can be corrected by more rehearsal.

Following the initial assignment in pantomime, subsequent assignments may be handled in exactly the same manner. Appropriate additions should be made to the basic character outline to meet the requirements of each new problem in pantomime. For each assignment the students must create a new character. In each case they must write a detailed plan for both the character and the action and rehearse it thoroughly before performing in class. Other suggested pantomimes may include the following:

> Character arriving at destination.
> Character handling an inanimate object.
> Character handling a living object.
> Character encountering a conflict that causes a change of mood.
> Character involved in a situation that tells a simple story.

As these pantomimes progress, students can be made aware of and begin to practice some of the important techniques of the actor's art— preparation, concentration, and the fundamentals of blocking.

Voice, Diction, and Oral Interpretation

Nowhere in the beginning drama class is the pressure of time more frustrating to the teacher than in the unit on voice, diction, and oral interpretation. There is time to do little more than to make each student aware of his individual weaknesses in this area, suggest exercises that can improve his voice and speech, and hope that he will practice them on his own time.

The Stage and the School contains an excellent chapter on voice and diction, which can be used to explain to students how speech is produced and how they may improve their own speech and voices. Several of the exercises in this chapter may be done in class to be sure that students understand them and execute them accurately.

If a tape recorder is available to the drama class, each student may be asked to bring in a prose selection about one minute long to read and record. As the tape is played back, each student can listen to and criticize his own reading, and with the help of the teacher select those exercises he should do to improve his own voice and diction. If time permits, it is interesting to allow each student to record the same material again near the end of the course so that he can see the improvement he has made.

In order to focus on phrasing, accuracy of sounds, and word coloring, students may be given assignments in oral interpretation of poetry. The chief pitfall, against which students must be warned, is that of over-emphasizing the rhythm and rhyme—commonly called sing-songing. A very useful technique to help students avoid this error in poetry reading is to require them to copy the poem in paragraph form, ignoring the lines of poetry, and read from that copy. Since students often groan at the mention of poetry, some attention must be given to the poetic selections they are asked to interpret. If they are to read poetry well, they must like it. In general, narrative poetry, didactic poetry, and dramatic mono-logues appeal to high school students, and lyric poetry bores them.

Current practices in teaching reading have discouraged oral reading, so students in a drama class often find it difficult to pronounce words correctly and phrase sentences intelligently when given their first assignments in oral interpretation. The lack of practice in reading aloud also causes them to be inhibited and nervous when asked to read to the entire class. They are afraid to dramatize and to characterize as they read. An excellent assignment to help student readers overcome their fears and communicate with their audience is to have each student read his favorite children's story to the class. Both the reader and the listeners, during this assignment, must transport themselves into a different environment—one in which the audience pretends to be young children and the reader pretends to be a teacher, parent, or baby-sitter, who must capture and maintain their attention. Most students are able to do this assignment well and to transfer much of what they learn in it to other assignments in oral interpretation.

Classroom Scenes

The techniques learned in earlier units of study can be combined in the performance of scenes from plays. These scenes should be approximately five minutes in length, should use only two characters, and should be selected by students from the plays that they have read and analyzed. That the actor must read and understand the entire play in order to portray a character in a portion of it is obvious. Therefore, students should be required to select scenes from plays on which they have previously reported. Although many books offer audition scenes for actors, none provide enough information about the plays and characters to give the actor a thorough understanding of the role he is to play.

Each of the four or five scenes that each student performs should be selected to present different acting problems. Each student should attempt to portray characters of different ages and different personalities, selected from as wide a range of types, styles, and periods of drama as possible. An interesting group of characters for a boy to attempt might include the Herdsman in *Oedipus Rex,* the Gravedigger in *Hamlet,* Romeo in *Romeo and Juliet,* John Proctor in *The Crucible,* and Henry in *The Skin of Our Teeth.* A girl might try Medea in *Medea,* Rosalind in *As You Like It,* Mrs. Malaprop in *The Rivals,* Emily in *Our Town,* and Eliza in *Look Homeward, Angel.*

For each scene they do, students should make a floor plan of the setting, plan the blocking, and rehearse the scene until it is thoroughly learned. Three or four days of class time should be ample for preparation of five minute scenes.

Although it is not possible for the teacher to direct each scene when ten or fifteen rehearsals are taking place simultaneously, he should comment on each scene as it is presented before the class and offer suggestions for improvement. The teacher should make detailed comments on at least one round of scenes, and instruct the students to conduct additional rehearsals and present the scenes a second time.

In the preparation and presentation of classroom scenes, as in other activities in the beginning drama class, the pressure of time is often frustrating. One must decide whether to have students work on one or two scenes until they are polished or to have them do several scenes, giving less time to each. As a rule, beginning students of acting seem to make more progress by doing several different characters than by studying a single character in depth.

CHAPTER **10**

Planning a Course
of Study for
Intermediate Drama

Among the students who take a beginning drama course, perhaps 25 or 30 percent will develop enough interest and skill that they will wish to continue their study of the theatre arts in an intermediate drama course. In addition to the student's own desire to pursue his theatre studies, the drama teacher should consider certain other qualifications or prerequisites for admission to the intermediate drama class. Earning a grade of "A" or "B" in the beginning drama class should be considered a minimum prerequiste to entering an intermediate class. Certainly students who have talent should be encouraged to enroll, but talent is so rare and indefinable that one cannot expect to fill a drama class with students who are talented. Intelligence may be more important than talent in achieving success in the theatre arts, and fortunately, most students who wish to continue their studies of drama have above average intelligence. Self-discipline and initiative are the most valuable qualities a student can bring to his work in theatre. Those beginning drama students who meet their assignments on time, who complete tasks without continual prodding and direction, and who organize their time and work well should be encouraged to enroll in an intermediate drama class.

Purposes of Intermediate Drama

The intermediate course in drama serves as a bridge between the beginning drama class, which focuses upon input to the individual students, and the play production class, which focuses upon output to the student audience. The beginning drama course gives the student background in theatre—its origin, development, literature, and performing techniques. The intermediate course in drama is designed to introduce the student to the production aspects of theatre—refined acting techniques, costuming, make-up, setting, lighting, and fully preparing a play for performance. When the student has completed this course, he is ready to participate in the play production class, in which the primary function is to produce plays for the high school student audience that will contribute to their cultural background and aesthetic experiences.

The major emphasis of the intermediate drama class is upon the development of student actors through the experience of performing before an audience in a theatre. Much that the actor must learn can be learned only by practicing his acting techniques in a play for an audience. The audience response, once he has become attuned to it, will tell the actor whether or not his characterization is believable, and whether or not he is projecting his role vocally, physically, and emotionally to his audience. In order to produce plays that will give them experience before an audience, students in the intermediate drama class must learn to handle the production crew assignments as well as the acting assignments of the plays they produce. The intermediate drama class should give students experiences in the totality of theatre as a performing, communicative art.

Materials and Texts

Since the intermediate drama class emphasizes the learning acquired through performance before an audience, the primary texts for the class will be the scripts of one-act plays. Exactly which scripts will be selected for production by each class will depend upon the students in that particular class. The teacher-director must select plays according to students' needs, abilities, limitations, and numbers. As nearly as possible, the criteria for play selection discussed in Chapter 13 should be followed. If the teacher wishes to have several copies of one-act play anthologies available for reading and consideration, *Thirty Famous One Act Plays*,[1] *24 Favorite One Act Plays*,[2] and *15 American One-Act Plays*[3] are excellent collections. Of course, not every play in these anthologies is appropriate for presentation in a high school. A selected list of one-act plays recommended for high school is included in the Appendix E of this book.

[1] *Thirty Famous One Act Plays,* ed. Bennett Cerf and Van H. Cartmell (Garden City, N.Y.: Garden City Publishing Co., 1943).
[2] *24 Favorite One Act Plays,* ed. Bennett Cerf and Van H. Cartmell (Garden City, N.Y.: Doubleday & Company, Inc., 1958).
[3] *15 American One-Act Plays,* ed. Paul Kozelka (New York: Washington Square Press, Inc., 1961).

Although there is no basic acting text available that is designed specifically for high school, any of the standard acting texts may be used as well in high school as in college. Miriam A. Franklin's *Rehearsal* [4] is among the most practical of these acting texts. Chapter 2, Business and Movement, is especially useful. Much rehearsal time will be saved if students study and master the rules and techniques in this chapter.

Activities and Assignments

The primary activity of the intermediate drama class is the production of one-act plays for presentation to an invited audience. These plays should be selected to provide at least one major role for each member of the class, so that each one has an opportunity to test his acting skills before an audience. The one-act plays can be rehearsed during the class period, for the most part, and presented for interested classes that meet for the same period of the day. A dozen classes of English or social studies students, with their teachers, may be invited to each of these performances. Since this plan causes no general interruption of the school schedule, the intermediate drama class can produce as many plays as it is able to handle.

It is of vital importance, both to the quality of the productions and to the progress of the students, that all plays be directed by the teacher. Although many more plays can be presented if directorial chores are assigned to students, a genuine concern for quality in education and in theatre should prohibit this practice. Students who have not yet participated in productions directed by a trained professional are hardly ready to assume the responsibilities of directing a show. If this practice of the blind leading the blind in theatrical productions exists at all, it should be left to neighborhood five-year-olds in the back yard, not brought into and encouraged by the schools. Teachers who believe that their student directors do as well or better than they could do in directing a play should reexamine their own training or their critical standards.

Those students who are not members of the cast may learn other aspects of production by being given crew assignments. A stage manager and assistant manager should be assigned to each play. It is their job to set up for each rehearsal, hold the script, check on the progress of crews, and run both the rehearsals and performance in an organizational and mechanical sense. The stage managers work very closely with the director, so experience in stage management is the best possible training for those students interested in learning to direct. Other students should be assigned to costume and property crews. Members of the costume crews should do any research needed to determine what costumes are

---

[4] Miriam A. Franklin, *Rehearsal: The Principles and Practice of Acting for the Stage,* 4th ed. (Englewood Cliffs, N.J.: Prentice-Hall, Inc., 1963).

appropriate for the play, and plan, and select or make the costumes. Likewise, the prop crew should research, plan, and select or make the props required.

Theatrical make-up should be a part of both the class instruction and the production activity of an intermediate drama class. The extent and practicality of the study of make-up depends on the school budget or the finances of the individual students. If possible, each student should have his own basic make-up kit. Several supply houses now offer student make-up kits for about five dollars each. As a minimum experience in make-up, the teacher should demonstrate both male and female straight and old age make-up, and then allow each student to try these two make-up problems on himself. Each student can acquire further experience in make-up by doing his own for each role he plays. Because of the students' limited experience, the teacher-director must closely supervise their work with make-up. A few general suggestions about make-up may be helpful to teachers. Skin problems are common to adolescents, and theatrical make-up tends to increase these problems. I have found it helpful to have students apply a thin layer of medicated base over clean skin before applying any theatrical make-up. Over this base, the tube-type grease paints, applied sparingly, make an excellent foundation for make-up. Stick-type make-up bases tend to be too dry over the medicated base, and rouges, shadows, lines, and highlights are difficult to apply and to blend over stick or pancake bases. Make-up over these drier bases does not set and last as well when powdered as it does over tube grease bases. The drier bases may be adequate for straight make-up, but are not desirable for character and age make-up.

Max Factor publishes a series of folders on make-up which is available for a small cost. These folders provide an excellent guide to almost any kind of make-up problem, and they can be obtained by individual students. Students enjoy doing make-up, and after a little practice, can do it very well.

As a supplement to the one-act plays presented, the intermediate drama class may also present poetry concerts, consisting of both choral and individual readings, as suggested in Chapter 7. A recent poetry concert at Canoga Park High School, for example, included choral readings of "General William Booth Enters Heaven," "Thirteen O'Clock," "Pershing At the Front," "Jabberwocky," "Silence"; excerpts from "The People, Yes"; and individual readings of "The Theatre Cat" from *archy and mehitabel*, "Nightmare Number Three," "On Friendship" from *The Prophet*, "How Do I Love Thee," "I've Never Seen A Moor," "Fire and Ice," and "Lucinda Matlock." Poetry programs should be given the same production attention—costumes, props, make up, and so on—that the one-act plays are given.

In addition to these production activities, students in an intermediate drama class should be given assignments in reading and research that further expand their knowledge of theatre. The study of Chapter II of *Rehearsal* has already been mentioned. It would be valuable to students to read the entire textbook, and class time may be found for discussion of some of the other chapters. If time permits, Chapter 1, "The Art of Acting"; Chapter 5, "Studying the Role"; Chapter 6, "Speak the Speech"; Chapter 8, "The Purposeful Pause"; and Chapter 12, "Creating a Character," are all worthy of class time.

Each student, individually or in collaboration with one other student, should be assigned to do some research and reading on some aspect of theatre and to present an oral report that occupies one full class period. For example, a particular historical period or nation might be assigned. Research could be done on the physical theatre, the social context, the style and types of plays that were popular, clothing of the era, and prominent playwrights of the time. A few outstanding plays should be read also. The oral report should include the research findings, and could be climaxed by the reading of a typical scene or two from plays of the period or nation.

Similarly, research on an important playwright might be assigned. Information should be gathered on his life, on the social conditions of his time, and on the theatre for which he wrote. All his major plays should be read. The oral report should include the information obtained and readings of excerpts from some of his plays.

Students of an intermediate drama class would be considerably enriched in their theatrical background if the following research reports were presented: Greek tragedy, religious drama of the Middle Ages, Restoration drama, Molière, Shaw, Ibsen, Wilder, O'Neill, Miller, and Wilde. Other areas that can be explored in this manner are costumes, dolls, actors and actresses, and scenic design.

Some schools may find it valuable, both in training intermediate drama students and in developing an *esprit de corps* among all drama students, to assign students from this class to crews for props, costumes, and promotion for the major productions of the play production class.

Along with the improvement of acting techniques, expansion of theatrical background, and introduction to production procedures, intermediate students of drama must learn the most important lesson of all, theatre discipline. Theatre discipline means responsibility to and for the entire group and whole production. It means attending school and rehearsals regularly. It means doing assigned tasks thoroughly and on time. Theatre discipline requires that any individual unable to accept his responsibilities, whether the reason be illness, incompetence, immaturity, or laziness, must be replaced by someone who can conform to the required discipline. The lessons of theatre discipline are often the most difficult lessons to learn and to teach.

CHAPTER 11

Planning a Course of Study for Play Production

The play production class is the high school's stock company of trained actors from among whom the casts of all major productions should be drawn. The purpose of the play production class is to present high quality theatrical performances that will enrich the cultural and aesthetic education of the student audience. If productions of high quality are to be achieved, the student actors admitted to the play production class must have demonstrated both their ability and their reliability by earning a grade of "A" or "B" in the intermediate drama class. Because the major process of determining student abilities and interests occurs in the beginning drama class, most students will earn good grades in the intermediate class and wish to continue in play production. Students should be permitted to repeat the play production class as many times as they wish, because the dramatic materials are different each time. The more talented students usually remain in play production as long as they are in high school, so the acting company of the class is made up of students with one, two, or three years of training and experience in theatre. Such a group of students can perform almost any play in a manner that will provide an exciting and worthwhile theatrical experience for the audience.

Closed Casting

The tradition of the senior class play, with open tryouts in which everyone has an equal opportunity to play a leading role, is so ingrained that even some well-trained high school directors follow this tradition. If drama is ever to make its optimum contribution to education, the senior play must be abandoned in favor of an organized class of trained student actors.

Simple logic, respect for the art of theatre, the self-respect of the teacher-director, and practicality demand that high school plays be cast with students in an advanced drama class. Those with training in theatre will be better actors than those without training. No one would suggest that open tryouts be held among the senior class to select members of the orchestra to play a symphony. Everyone from the custodian, to the music teacher, to the principal, has more respect for the art of music than to do such a thing. Yet the quality of music produced by an untrained orchestra is no worse than the quality of theatre produced by an untrained cast. The drama teacher who is willing to direct a senior play is announcing in effect, that there is no need to have classes in drama, or at least that drama classes and the production of plays are unrelated. For reasons of self-preservation in the educational establishment, as well as personal ego, I should hate to admit that students with no training could perform as well as those whom I had taught for a year or two! Finally, students whose participation in a play is part of a class for which they will receive credit and a grade will rehearse more seriously and effectively than those who have volunteered for an extracurricular activity.

Activities and Assignments

The production of one or two full-length plays each semester is the major activity of the play production class. In addition, students in this advanced drama class may do concert readings of plays, plays and scenes for interscholastic contests, individual recitals of plays, and cuttings of plays, novels, and poetry. The extent of these other dramatic activities depends upon the size and quality of the class as well as the school calendar.

The major play to be produced cannot be selected until class has begun, because the specific student actors available must be considered. Although it is seldom possible to find a play in which every student in the class may have a role, it is desirable to find one which uses as many of them as possible. During the first few weeks of the class, students may participate in the play selection process by reading plays suggested by the teacher-director or members of the class and reporting their evaluation to the group. Given the general standards for play selection discussed in Chapter 13, students can make a valuable contribution to the selection process. Of course, the final determination must be made by the teacher-director. In fairness to the students, the teacher-director should indicate at the outset that he must make the final decision, but that he wants the suggestions, opinions, and reactions of students to help him in the selection.

The process of producing a play will be discussed in detail in Chapter 15, but some questions regarding selection of the cast arise here. Although a good director does not select a play unless he has actors in mind who can play the most difficult roles, precasting is unfair to the actors, the production, and the director. In other words, the director should have the advantage of knowing that John could play Hamlet, if no one else in the class gave a better reading during tryouts. Every member of the class should be encouraged to try out for every role which he thinks he might be able to play. All students should, of course, have ample opportunity to read the play and to practice reading the roles in which they are interested, before trying out for the director. This author has been mistaken in prejudgment of a student actor's ability often enough to realize the importance of keeping an open mind at all casting tryouts. A girl who had been almost impossible to direct as the Fortune Teller in *The Skin of Our Teeth* and seemed incapable of projecting any kind of characterization wanted to try out for the Nurse in Jeffers' *Medea*. For the sake of fairness, she was allowed to read. Her reading gave the character ancient wisdom, power, pathos, and beauty. She was cast, and played the role so well that when directing a professional production of the same play a few years later, it was difficult to find an actress whose interpretation of the Nurse was as satisfying.

Just as the teacher-director must be willing to cast every student in the role he reads best, so every student in the class must be willing to accept the role in which he is cast, whether it be the lead, the butler, or an offstage voice. There is no place in a play production group for the spoiled brat who demands his own way about everything. Let him take his toys and go home!

Double-casting of the roles in each play has been a traditional practice in many high schools. On the list of what to avoid in high school drama, double-casting should come right after the senior play. Those who advocate double-casting argue that it is more democratic because it gives more students an opportunity to participate. Why democracy is brought into the argument is not quite clear, but it is clear that selecting a play with a larger cast or doing two plays instead of one would also give more students an opportunity to participate. Advocates of double-casting also point out that it provides insurance against illnesses and emergencies among the cast—someone is ready to step into every role. A better solution to cover emergencies, borrowed from the professional theatre, is to assign two fairly versatile actors, one male and one female, to be stage managers for the show and to act as general understudies for all roles. Since these stage managers must attend all rehearsals, follow the prompt book, and walk through the parts of actors who are absent, it is fairly easy for them to step into any role.

It is inconceivable that one could ever find two equally good casts for the same play at the same time in any high school. Being designated second-best as a member of the second cast of a play would not seem to be a valuable educational experience for any student. At the very least, the director who double casts his show must either put in twice as much rehearsal time or be content with half as good a show. It would be far more sensible to spend the additional time rehearsing a second show, one selected to suit the talents of the students available for casting in it.

Concert readings of plays can provide valuable experiences for both student actors and audiences, without requiring the detailed organization, high budget, and extended rehearsal time involved in a fully produced play. Concert readings can be presented on a bare stage in front of a cyclorama or curtain and require only a few stools and music stands. Use of risers and pin spots may add to the effectiveness of these readings. Advanced students who have expressed an interest in directing may be asigned to direct concert readings, under the close supervision of the teacher-director. Because the first responsibility is to the audience, the teacher must be sure that the student director is doing a good job. Some student directors will need almost no help, while others will need to confer with the teacher after every rehearsal.

Most plays will need to be adapted slightly if they are to be read instead of staged, and some may require that narration be added to replace the elements of scenery and action. Regardless of the number of characters in the play selected, only about six actors should appear in each concert reading. Each actor should have two or three characters to read, and some minor characters may be eliminated entirely. The challenge of portraying several roles in the same play without the aid of make-up, costume, or movement is excellent training for student actors. They must learn to use their voices, facial expressions, and gestures to show the differences in characters.

Almost any play can be adapted for a concert reading, and the selections will depend primarily upon the audiences to whom they will be presented. Plays about historical incidents or social issues, for example, could be offered for social studies classes, and plays that appear in their textbooks could be read to English classes. Other plays, which could not be done effectively as fully staged productions, can be presented as concert readings. *The Amen Corner* and *Raisin in the Sun,* for example, require all Negro casts and could not be convincing if done in black face, yet they say things which should be heard and understood by students in an all-white school. *A Majority of One* requires so many sets that it is prohibitive, either physically or financially, in many schools. *Barefoot in Athens* has so few roles for girls that most schools would not wish to do it as a major production. Likewise, *Saint Joan, Elizabeth the Queen, The Lark,* and *Inherit the Wind* have predominantly male casts. All these plays could be done as concert readings, requiring only ten or twelve rehearsals, and all have a place in educational theatre.

Interscholastic play tournaments and acting contests have genuine value to students and teachers of high school drama, in spite of the fact that the importance of winning can easily be overemphasized. The value of contests lies in the opportunities they afford student actors to perform before an audience of strangers, to see the work of drama students from other schools, to compare their own acting techniques with those of other students, and to become acquainted with students from other places who share their interest in theatre. Although the same materials that students prepare for interscholastic contests could doubtless be prepared for presentation within their own school, the excitement of competition heightens their motivation and improves the quality of their performances. Students who are entering contests, either individually or in a play, should certainly have the benefit of faculty direction of their entries, so that they may do full justice to themselves and their scripts.

It is the responsibility of the teacher-director to put the competitive aspects of these tournaments in proper perspective before taking students to them. First, students should understand that judgment of the performances is subjective. Who wins may depend as much upon the individual taste of the judges as upon the quality of the performances. A group doing "The Old Lady Shows Her Medals" for a judge who dislikes J. M. Barrie's sentimental comedy might not stand a chance of winning. A judge who has played or directed *Hamlet* might not be objective about any interpretation that varied from his own. In order to develop their own critical standards, as well as to remove some of the sting from defeat and some of the inflation from victory, students can be instructed to make their own evaluations and ratings of each performance before the decision of the judges is announced. Student ratings can form the basis for very interesting and instructive discussion on the way home from the contest.

Those students and teachers who like to win, or who need to win to gain recognition in their own schools, would do well to select material that concentrates on highly theatrical spectacle—violent emotions, elaborate scenery, colorful costumes, complicated movement. If they were competing in high school tournaments, David Belasco would win more often than Constantin Stanislavski!

As a final project in the play production class, each student may be asked to do a reading of a play for the entire class. The plays to be read may be assigned by the teacher-director or selected by the students with his approval. Each student must cut his play to forty-five minutes of reading time, write the narration needed, and read all the roles. The assignment is stimulating to the performers, and serves to broaden the knowledge of dramatic literature for the entire class.

In addition to these assignments as actors and stage managers, students in play production may have to do crew assignments on props, costumes, publicity, and promotion. To what extent play production students do this work depends upon how much crew work is taken over by students in an intermediate drama class. In play production, as in intermediate drama, actors should apply their own make-up.

Effect of Play Production

Without elaborate and expensive follow-up studies, it is impossible to know what effect the exposure to good theatre has upon the student audience, but it is reasonable to assume that they will benefit by it.

It is possible to obtain information about the effect of the play production program upon the participants by framing a discussion question that will stimulate them to summarize their understanding of theatre. Students should not be given advance notice of the question. They should be told that the question will not be graded, because its purpose is to evaluate the course rather than the individual students. One such question on which play production students were asked to write for a class hour was: Discuss your ideas and opinions about the place and importance of theatre—personally, socially, and educationally. Following are excerpts from typical student essays.

> Socially the play serves many purposes: entertaining, serves as a standardizer, but most important, a way for carrying out man's constant and incessant desire to express himself. . . . Educationally—I believe that here lies the real value of the theatre. It has served for thousands of years in this sense. It is actually the only vicarious education there is. It serves to familiarize people with others' lives and problems, through experiencing them yourself. It can have great psychological effects on a person, and maybe give them insight into their own problems. Educationally—political strifes, history, great literary works, development of thoughts, becoming familiar with other cultures and customs can all be expressed with a purpose. . . . Personally—the theatre is to me understanding humanity. I'm not interested in it because I desire an escape from my problems or life, but because I believe life to be so short to become familiarized with all its facets, and because reading, and understanding authors' impressions of people and *being* one of those people is developing and training yourself to become acquainted with the intricate and infinite instrument we all have—the human mind. To understand completely this mind is to understand life—a thing which I would very much like to accomplish. I realize this is *impossible* but through the theatre I am able to understand more and more. . . . I think that a playwright has the responsibility of writing plays always with a purpose that will be not only entertaining but educational and lasting.

This was written by a girl who was about to graduate. She was a student leader, a foreign language major, and had been taking drama for two years. Another girl who had been in drama classes for two years and was a junior had this comment.

> The theatre is a place where, whether spectator or participant, a person can become a part of some situation completely different than their own. You can feel emotions of someone you have never known or of some great person who has passed away. I feel that the theatre is educational in that it brings important ideas into view so that even the most illiterate person is capable of understanding them.... The theatre is a place where people can expand their ideas. They can lose themselves in something worthwhile.

A shy boy who was about to graduate and who had been too inhibited to play any but minor roles wrote the following:

> Theatre to me is the embodiment of man's spirit, the materialization of man's moral and spiritual ideas, and a showcase to display the growth of man's spirit. The theatre has a definite place in society. Aside from being a place of entertainment, the theatre, whether movie house or legitimate, is a place of worship, as all tribute to art is a tribute to God. To some it is a dream world, a world of escape, a place to forget troubles and come away refreshed. To others it is a place to learn. Socially, the theatre is a meeting place, a gathering of people to respond to a playwright's work and to the performers.... The theatre has a profound effect on all phases of life. In government, it can influence or steer a group into believing or thinking alike. In society, it can introduce new styles, manners, and customs, and it can teach a person something. Everyone who has ever gone to a theatre has come away influenced one way or the other. As for myself, the experience ... has brought me rich rewards. I have acquired poise, and a personality has begun to develop. I know that I am not an actor and probably never will be, but the experience has become an important period in my development. From its earliest form, the theatre has been an integral part of the progress of man as a society and as an individual.

A rebel who created problems in routine classes in school, but was able to conform to the discipline of all classes in order to retain the privilege of remaining in drama, wrote the following reply:

> Personally, this is a part of self-expression which is essentially important to my physical and mental health. This could sound very funny but it isn't. For people who are creative, there is something to be expressed all the time. Some people have a musical talent in which they lose themselves temporarily. Naturally this releases emotional tension. At the same time, this release is put into a constructive way. Individuals who are creative express themselves differently. Some lean toward sculpture, others, acting. I like to paint as well as act, regardless of what talent I may have. Being on the stage basically shows the audience what I know, and at the same time gives me a great deal of satisfaction in knowing I'm entertaining

(Theoretically I could be making a brash statement) however, I do enjoy it. But if I don't release it, it builds up, and comes out quite on the negative side.

Finally, another boy, whose interest in theatre was difficult to understand because he was too shy to express it in any kind of performance, made this reply.

> Theatre is, and always has been, one of the most important institutions of society. One of the primary purposes of theatre has been to instruct people in the why and wherefore of human existence—to instruct them, that is, through a medium in which ordinarily complex ideas become more or less digestible. The plays of the ancient Greeks helped familiarize the people with their gods and history. The miracle, mystery, and morality plays in the Middle Ages taught the people about saints, Biblical characters, and moral standards of living. The theatre, in these instances, was more than just a place for entertainment—it was as important in the lives of people as their churches and schools. This is what the theatre is, or should be, today. It should serve the purpose of filtering to the public in the form of entertainment, some of the problems that are troubling the world today.

High school students whose experience in play production has helped them develop the kind of perception that these statements indicate may well help to solve some of the problems that are troubling the world today.

CHAPTER **12**

Planning a
Course of Study
for Stagecraft

The multiple nature of the stagecraft class—partly mechanics, partly art, partly drama, and partly service—creates many problems.

Who is to teach stagecraft? Ideally, of course, every high school should have a trained technical director, but only a few large high schools in wealthy suburban areas can afford to hire a specialist in stagecraft. A teacher of industrial arts can handle the construction of scenery and the maintenance of sound and electrical equipment on the stage, but he seldom has any interest in or sensitivity to the artistic elements of stagecraft—color, line, mood, and timing of cues. The drama teacher may have greater knowledge of the artistic elements, but still be unable to design and paint a set or avoid overloading dimmer circuits and blowing up the switchboard. The art teacher may be no better a mechanic than the drama teacher, and may also find production schedules frustrating. Which of these three partially qualified teachers should handle stagecraft depends upon which one is willing to assume the responsibility and learn the part of the job he does not know. Because he has the greatest stake in the success of the stagecraft class, the drama teacher is often the one who teaches it.

The selection of both students and curriculum for stagecraft is affected by the service responsibilities of the class. In addition to providing technical facilities and crews for plays produced by the high school, they must provide them for all of the assemblies, concerts, and programs presented in the school's auditorium. The preparation for and operation of all of these auditorium activities leaves little time for formal classroom instruction in stagecraft. Students are taught the various aspects of stagecraft as the demand for the knowledge arises from the production schedule. This constant need for crews to operate programs often requires that stagecraft students be taken out of classes, and that they work on stage after school hours. Students accepted for enrollment in a stagecraft class must, therefore, be sufficiently conscientious and capable so that they can maintain a satisfactory academic standing in spite of the missed classes and extended after-school hours which the class requires of them. It is also essential that they be honest and that they learn to be careful, reliable, and self-disciplined. The value and portability of the tools and equipment with which stagecraft students work makes honesty an important prerequisite for the course. The physical facilities are such that the instructor cannot guard all equipment at all times. Power tools, catwalks, counterweights, and electricity are all potentially dangerous, and stagecraft students must learn to be extremely careful in working with them. They must also learn to be reliable in locking doors and cabinets, putting tools and equipment away, and keeping track of keys. Stagecraft students must learn self-discipline, because it is impossible for the instructor to supervise individual students.

Because the stagecraft class in most high schools is a working service crew rather than a traditional class, the enrollment should not exceed fifteen students, and each student should be approved by the teacher before he is permitted to enroll.

Materials, Texts, and Equipment

If a textbook for stagecraft is authorized, Herbert V. Hake's *Here's How, A Guide to Economy in Stagecraft*,[1] is an excellent simplified text. This book emphasizes diagrams, with a minimum of written explanation, and is therefore a quick, easy source of information about how to construct or rig scenery for the stage. In this case, truly, one picture is worth a thousand words! If it is not possible to give every student a copy of this text, it should certainly be available in the scene shop for reference. The other essential reference work for stagecraft is Stanley McCandless, *A Method of Lighting the Stage*,[2] the standard definitive work on stage lighting. Two additional useful reference books for stagecraft are *Play Production*[3] and *Stagecraft and Scene Design*.[4]

[1] Herbert V. Hake, *Here's How, A Guide to Economy in Stagecraft* (New York: Samuel French, Inc., 1958).

[2] Stanley MCAndless, *A Method of Lighting the Stage*, Rev. ed. (New York: Theatre Arts, Inc., 1939).

[3] Hennings Nelms, *Play Production* (New York: Barnes & Noble, Inc., 1958).

[4] Herbert Philippe, *Stagecraft and Scene Design* (Boston: Houghton Mifflin Company, 1953).

Standard carpenter's and electrician's hand tools are needed for stage-craft, along with whatever lumber, muslin, and hardware the current projects require. Specifications of the materials needed for various kinds of scenery construction are given in the texts mentioned.

Stagecraft Actiivties

Members of the stagecraft class must begin their training by learning the vocabulary, geography, and operation of the theatre. Specific equipment varies considerably from school to school, but most will have some kind of sound system, electrical switchboard, and stage rigging. Students are fascinated by all this equipment, and motivation is no problem in teaching them how to use it.

The requirements of set construction will vary according to the plays selected, and much set work in the high school consists of rebuilding and repainting, rather than new construction. Nevertheless, stagecraft students should learn to build such basic units as flats, doors, windows, arches, ground rows, platforms, and steps. They should also learn how to cover, size, paint, and fireproof scenery, as well as how to mount it and shift it on the stage.

In order to light the various programs and plays effectively, students need to understand the uses, operation, and maintenance of the various lighting instruments available to them. Most high school stages have ellipsoidal reflector spotlights, baby spots with plano-convex or Fresnel lenses, floodlights, and strip lights. Students should learn the various kinds of lamps used in these instruments according to wattage, shape, size, and base. They should also learn how to make a light plot. In order to do this, they must learn not only the uses of the lighting instruments, but also the use of color in lighting and the load each circuit will handle. The basic information which students need about stage lighting is contained in the McCandless book, but they will soon discover that much of the art of lighting is trial and error. When the light plot is made and the instruments are placed and focused in advance, much rehearsal time will be saved. It will still be necessary, however, to make changes and adjustments during rehearsals.

Organization of Stagecraft

The heavy schedule of activities in the high school auditorium demands that the teacher of stagecraft organize and schedule his and the students' time rather carefully. Members of the stagecraft class may be divided into three crews—lights, sound, and stage. Likewise, the term may be divided into three equal time periods, and the three crews may rotate, so that each crew spends one third of the term on lights, one third on sound, and one third on stage. The entire class should be members of the shop crew at all times so that they are available for building and painting whenever there is work to be done.

During the regular stagecraft class period of fifty or sixty minutes, very little construction can be done because so much time is consumed getting tools and materials out and putting them away. Stagecraft students should be required to work in the shop after school, and a log of the time each student spends, along with the work he does, should be kept. The after-school time spent working in the shop and at rehearsals can be required of students in lieu of homework and used as the basis for a grade in stagecraft.

Not all members of the crews will be required for each program, and the program will operate more smoothly if there are no unoccupied crew members present. In order to distribute the crew assignments evenly and to be certain that a crew member doesn't miss the same class too often, a calendar of crew assignments, listing dates, periods, and names should be kept.

Students often become so involved in and dedicated to their work in stagecraft that they neglect their other school studies. In stagecraft, as in play production, it seems a good policy to limit participation to those students who maintain passing grades in all their studies. Few, if any, students will be lost to stagecraft because of this policy, and many will improve their grades considerably. In order to enforce the policy, students may be asked to circulate grade slips to their teachers every four or five weeks. Those whose grades are not satisfactory may be placed on probation and transferred to a study hall for a couple of weeks. If their grades improve, they may return to stagecraft; if not, they are dropped from the class.

The rules for eligibility for stage crew at Canoga Park High School and the manner in which they were developed seem significant enough to justify telling another personal experience. Several years ago, I was forced to teach the stagecraft class, because everyone else refused to do it. The class was made up entirely of boys, most of whom had had minor problems with the disciplinary rules and academic standards of the school. Some of them had worked on stage crews for plays I had directed, and although they thought it strange that a woman should teach stagecraft, they were willing to give me a chance. I asked them to elect a crew manager who was to be in full charge of the class, as long as they got their work done and did not violate school rules. I added one rule. No student was to be taken out of a class in which he was failing to work on the stage. The boys chose their leader well and soon asked if they could establish rules for eligibility for stage crew. They were given permission, provided that their rules were approved by me and by the administration, because we would have to enforce them. They investigated the rules for athletes and student officers and made their own a little higher. In order to be on the stage crew, a student could not have any failing grades nor any unsatisfactory marks in citizenship, and no more than one "D" grade. The students also established the probationary period in study hall and the drop from stagecraft for students whose grades did not improve. These rules have worked so well that my job as teacher consists of checking to see that work is done properly, and occasionally showing students how to do something.

Design

Stage design and decoration can be best handled by an art teacher and art students. Many art departments offer classes in stage design that provide designs and construction plans for all school productions. Stage design classes, like stagecraft classes, seldom have time to learn theories and practices of theatrical design, except in the process of providing an appropriate environment for the plays being produced by the high school.

As soon as a play is selected, copies should be given to the design teacher and his students. The director should confer with the designers to explain his interpretation of the play, his concept of style, and any obligatory physical requirements of the setting. The design students then read the play and do appropriate research of the style, architecture, and decor that the play requires. With this background, they develop designs and floor plans, which are submitted to the director for his selection.

In schools that have no stage design class, the director is responsible for the design of the sets. He may create an original design, copy one used in a professional production, or modify the original setting in some way, depending on his individual knowledge and skill. Whether the design comes from the director or the stage design class, the stagecraft class is responsible for its construction and operation. Since most high schools have limited stage facilities, great ingenuity is needed in designing and building multiple set shows. Hinges, wheels, double-faced flats, and units will be the stagecraft teacher's greatest friends when a play requires several set changes. Small sets can be built on low platforms with wheels and rolled into place quickly. Reversible screens or book flats can be turned around to change sets. Two-, three-, or four-sided set units can be mounted on wheels, turned, and regrouped to form several different scenes. Ingenuity and imagination can compensate for many inadequacies of high school stages.

The photographs on the following pages illustrate some of the methods that may be employed to mount plays requiring several changes of setting on a limited stage. The photographs are of productions at Canoga Park High School. The stage has a usable proscenium width of thirty feet and a height of fourteen feet. It is twenty-five feet from the curtain to the rear wall, with an apron area in front of the curtain of six feet. There is only three feet of wing space on each side of the stage, but this may be increased slightly by adjusting the tormentors. There is no gridiron or counterweight equipment. Curtains are hung from steel beams ten feet above the teaser. There is no scene shop or dock, and the largest door onto the stage is five and one-half feet wide and seven feet high. Because of these limitations, all scenery and furniture to be used in a play must either remain on stage during the entire show or be small enough to be moved through a door.

For *She Stoops to Conquer,* the playing area was expanded by putting platforms in the orchestra pit which extended the apron an additional six feet. Ornamental facsimiles of the footlights of the period were placed around the perimeter of this apron in order to relate it to the set used on stage. The profiles of the wings were cut in perspective to enhance the illusion of depth created by the perspective painting of the backdrop. The apron also contributed to the presentational style required by this play, by allowing the actors to come closer to the audience for their asides.

FIGURE 1 *She Stoops to Conquer*

Family Portrait shows another way in which the orchestra pit may be used as an acting area. In this play, the garden of Mary and Joseph's home in Nazareth, with the carpenter's shop on one side and the house on the other, is the setting for several scenes throughout the play, while the other sets (a wine shop, a street, a public well, and the Upper Room) are used only once each. Building the garden set on one-foot risers in the orchestra pit, with the house at the left of the proscenium arch and the shop at the right, made it possible to leave it in place throughout the show. The other sets could be put in place behind the closed curtain while scenes in the garden were being played. The wall and gate at the front edge of the stage folded to the floor when that set was not in use. The photographs show the orchestra pit set and the detail of the areas at the left and right.

Figure 2 *Family Portrait*

Figure 3 *Family Portrait*

FIGURE 4   *Family Portrait*

The settings for *Romeo and Juliet* were given unity by the false proscenium, which framed the stage with an Italian Renaissance arch. The set was made up of three large units, each of which had three or four different sides and was mounted on wheels, as were the smaller set pieces, the fountain, and wall sections. These units could be turned and regrouped to form the seven different sets used in this production of

FIGURE 5   *Romeo and Juliet*

Romeo and Juliet. Three of these sets are shown in these photographs: Juliet's garden and balcony, the street in Verona, and the Capulet's ballroom.

FIGURE 6 *Romeo and Juliet*

FIGURE 7 *Romeo and Juliet*

Six three-dimensional reversible units formed most of the two settings for *The Importance of Being Earnest*. The double door at stage right, which is recessed for the interior set used in the first act, is flush with the wall and topped with a decorative gable for the exterior setting used in the second and third acts. The same units, reversed, form the left and right sides of both sets. The upstage wall and fireplace of Act I are replaced by the gazebo up center.

Mounting three-dimensional units on wheels and placing sandbags inside of them keeps the units stable without the use of stage braces. Note that in *The Importance of Being Earnest,* as in *Romeo and Juliet,* the independent units are placed so that they overlap or meet to form jogs, niches, and alcoves rather than straight walls. This placement not only

FIGURE 8   *The Importance of Being Earnest*

FIGURE 9   *The Importance of Being Earnest*

makes the sets more interesting visually, but also conceals the seams where units join together.

Simple backgrounds for the skits in *A Thurber Carnival* were provided on two revolving turntables, which were framed by a false proscenium decorated with Thurber-like cartoons. Each of the turntables accomodated six backgrounds on panels hinged to a central post. The first photograph shows the turntables with matching backgrounds for "Gentlemen Shoppers." The second reveals the stage right turntable with a neutral backing to focus attention upon the masks used for "The Wolf at the Door," and the third suggests a tropical island for "Casuals of the Keys." The turntables are eight feet in diameter. The tops are ¾-inch plywood semicircles joined together with strap iron. There are twelve, three-inch swivel wheels bolted around the perimeter of each. They have a floor flange mounted in the center, and pivot easily in a slightly larger

FIGURE 10 *A Thurber Carnival*

FIGURE 11 *A Thurber Carnival*

floor flange mounted on the stage floor. The wheels are masked with masonite tacked to the edges of the plywood tops. They require no

FIGURE 12 *A Thurber Carnival*

frame and can easily be revolved manually by one person, even when two or three actors are "riding" the turntable.

A wagon stage, patterned after those of the late Middle Ages and used throughout *Hamlet,* is another example of a simple and versatile unit of scenery. In the first photograph, it is placed at the extreme left of the

FIGURE 13 *Hamlet*

stage and is completely bare so that the sky cyclorama may be seen through it. It suggests an outdoor locale for Polonius to bid farewell to

Laertes. For the gravedigger scene, an iron picket fence is placed on the wagon to suggest a church yard. The grave is in the orchestra pit be-

FIGURE 14 *Hamlet*

FIGURE 15 *Hamlet*

cause the stage has no trap door. In the third picture, the wagon has been moved three feet nearer stage center to serve as Gertrude's chamber, an ornate drapery has been hung on the upstage side of the wagon to provide a hiding place for Polonius, and a stool has been placed on the platform. In the last photograph, the wagon has been pushed left so that half of it is offstage (remember the three feet of wing space!), and it forms part of the palace hall in which the players perform for the court. Because this wagon unit was only moved laterally, it was mounted on wheels that did not turn.

FIGURE 16   *Hamlet*

These five photographs of *Liliom* illustrate the simplest and most inexpensive device of all for staging a multiple set show—set pieces, props,

FIGURE 17   *Liliom*

FIGURE 18   *Liliom*

furniture, and book flats, backed by a sky cyclorama. The first set has only a bench, a street lamp, a tree, and a ground row to represent the park. Next, book flats, a cot and a tripod suggest the photo studio. The railroad embankment is made of standard stage platforms covered with chicken wire and muslin with a signal light at stage left. In the fourth picture, a white panel mounted on a platform and three white stools are

FIGURE 19   *Liliom*

used for the heavenly court. The last photograph is of Julie's yard, which is suggested by a picket fence, a bench, and a table and chairs.

FIGURE 20 *Liliom*

FIGURE 21 *Liliom*

The portal set for *The Crucible,* shown in the following pictures, provided a very simple, appropriate, and economical setting for the play. A framework of heavy, rough beams, backed by a black cyclorama, was

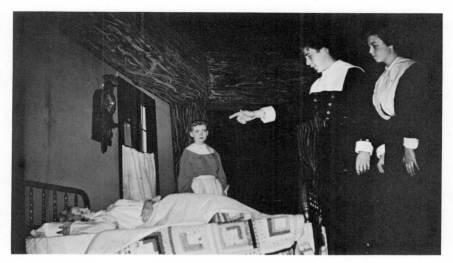

FIGURE 22 *The Crucible*

used for the entire production. Simple units inserted in the open portals gave specificity to each locale. A wall with a window and clock represents Betty's bedroom. A fireplace and picnic table suggest Proctor's kitchen. A high judge's bench and rough chairs are used for the courtroom.

FIGURE 23 *The Crucible*

FIGURE 24 *The Crucible*

Finally, black bars and a ball and chain create a stark prison for the last scene of *The Crucible*.

FIGURE 25 *The Crucible*

CHAPTER 13

Selection of Plays for High School Production

Among the problems facing the secondary school drama director, perhaps the most difficult and persistent is that of selecting the right plays for production. Since respect for the entire secondary school drama program, and even its right to survival in public schools, may depend upon finding a satisfactory solution to this problem, some standards or guideposts to help the director select plays that will stimulate the growth of theatre arts in the secondary schools are suggested here.

That neither actor nor director can be better than the script of the play with which he works must constantly be borne in mind by the director as he considers plays for production. Many of us have delighted at the skill and charm of the Lunts, or other theatrical greats, in mediocre vehicles. But even great talent added to masterful technique cannot overcome poor material, and few high schools are blessed with genius in either actors or director!

General Requirements of the Play Script

Given an adequately trained director and students of average ability, training, and experience, three general requirements may be demanded of the plays chosen for production. They must be worth doing for an artistic director. They must be worth playing for student actors. They must be worth witnessing for the audience.

Director's Requirements

What qualities must a play possess in order to challenge the artistic high school director throughout the long rehearsal period? A director will spend from four to eight weeks producing a full-length play. He will spend approximately one hundred hours in actual rehearsal, and an untold number of hours working alone with the script. In this length of time, a thin play becomes threadbare, and a director who has spent five or six hours teaching adolescents before he begins his daily rehearsal is apt to nod and nap, while his students rehearse, if tedium is heaped upon fatigue. Therefore, the play must first of all be one on which the director is completely sold—one which will make him look forward to each rehearsal with genuine enthusiasm.

The teacher who is competent both as a director and an educator will require that every script he selects have some worthy educational purpose. Specifically, its purpose will be either to educate, to present a problem, or to entertain. More often than not, a play will serve more than one of these purposes, and every play *must* entertain if it is to communicate.

Let the director, even in educational theatre, always remember that entertainment is a worthy objective for his program, especially in times when emotional tension is high. Plays whose primary purpose is to entertain may be divided into two categories: those which amuse and those which offer escape. Farces, light comedies, imaginative fantasies, mysteries, and melodramas are often designed only to entertain an audience. Such plays as *Kind Lady, Ladies in Retirement, Night Must Fall, The Importance of Being Earnest, Clarence, Master Pierre Patelin, Harvey, She Stoops to Conquer, The School for Scandal, The Taming of the Shrew, As You Like It,* and *What Every Woman Knows,* whose primary purpose is to entertain, may all be considered worthy material for high school presentation. They also have other values that make them suitable for school productions.

Plays that present a problem are the most difficult to find because many such plays deal with highly controversial subject matter. By definition, such plays must treat a problem that is both important and unsolved. Even though the ideal problem play will only offer arguments on each side of an issue, without advocating a definite solution, members of the community, who have taken sides and become emotionally as well as intellectually involved in the problem dealt with on the stage, may accuse the school of advocating an idea which they oppose and which is therefore detrimental to young minds. Then the fireworks begin! Nevertheless, there are plays dealing with common individual or social problems, rather than religious, economic, or partisan political ones, which can and should be included in the secondary school production schedule. The problem play should stimulate the participants and the audience to investigate, discuss, and analyze the issues presented. What more worthy objective is there for a production of a play by a school?

Even with the limitations of subject matter imposed upon high school productions of problem plays, many solid, dramatic, and vital plays from this category remain for selection. Among these are *Dear Brutus, Outward Bound, The Cradle Song, State of the Union, You Can't Take it With You, The Crucible, Winterset, Shadow and Substance, Liliom, Saint Joan, R.U.R.,* and *Raisin in the Sun.* Of course, certain minor cutting is required in many of these scripts before they may be presented in most high schools, but it seems well worth the effort when the reward is an opportunity to stimulate young people to think about such problems as whether people could improve with a second chance, what constitutes a happy life, what is justice, whether all races are equal, or whether honesty in politics can be achieved.

Although the theatre, whether commercial, community, or educational, should never become a podium for pedagogy, plays that combine educational with dramatic values should have priority in high schools. There are many theatrically sound plays whose greatest value is educational. Plays which deal with historical incidents, those which are biographical, those which introduce other nations, eras, or strata of society, and those which dramatize the great truths of established moral and social laws may all serve to educate. Certainly, a balanced high school program will include some plays with educational values. *Cyrano De Bergerac, Family Portrait, Lady Precious Stream, Harriet, Abe Lincoln in Illinois, I Remember Mama, Little Women, The Romancers, Sun-Up, Icebound, Tillie the Mennonite Maid, Papa Is All, Mary of Scotland, The Doctor In Spite of Himself, The Imaginary Invalid, Elizabeth the Queen, Our Town, The Barretts of Wimpole Street, Pygmalion,* and *The Skin of Our Teeth* all have educational value—either historical, biographical, or social.

The director should also require that the play selected be good theatre: that is, it must present a question that interests the audience; it must have strong dramatic value in its action, conflict, and emotional portrayal; it must also have literary value in its theme, structure, and dialogue. Any play that contains these elements of good theatre is certain to stimulate the director to his best efforts in shaping a good production.

Finally, the director must choose a play that challenges his own creative abilities—his perception and imagination. The talent of the director will be demonstrated, as he works with the problems of staging, setting, lighting, costuming, and interpretation to create a show that is consistent and unified and artistic. He will find it exciting to combine these elements to create the dominant mood required by the particular script. Since the director is responsible for achieving variety in pace, timing, and mood—for giving light and shade to the production—he must select a play that will allow him to be a creative as well as an interpretative artist.

Sutton Vane's *Outward Bound,* for example, stimulates both the creative and interpretative talents of the director. The design of the setting will depend upon the director's approach to the play. He may choose to surround his cast with an impressionistic ship's lounge, which is as ephemeral as the moment between life and death in which the play occurs, or he may prefer a detailed, realistic setting, against which the characters will stand out in bold relief. In the blocking of action, in pace, and in timing, the director will be challenged as he moves his actors from the casual holiday-like cruise atmosphere of the first act, into the tense realization of their destination during the second act, and finally to the meeting with the kindly Examiner at the Port of Eternity in the third act. Because each of the several characters is equally important and has a separate story to unfold, the director will find it exciting to keep the various complications, crises, and resolutions in perfect balance and still avoid monotony in pace and mood. If each story follows the same pattern in its interpretation and intensity, the later ones will be less effective than the earlier ones, and the show will drag. The director must select his major climax and guide his production toward that high point. *Outward Bound* is so well balanced that any one of several characters may be considered to be the protagonist, as illustrated by the fact that three separate, successful professional productions have placed star players in each of the roles of Tom Pryor, Mrs. Midget, and the pair of lovers, Henry and Ann. It should perhaps be mentioned here that in this play, as in many others, the director may make a choice of several styles of interpretation, according to his choice of protagonist, without distorting the author's intent in the play. It is the director's job to understand the playwright's ideas and to clarify them for the actors and audience but not to change the playwright's meaning to suit his own design. If the director does not like or agree with what is said in a given play, he should abandon its production rather than change its meaning. He can then find another play, which says what he wants to communicate to an audience.

Actor's Requirements

Student actor's abilities and demands must also be considered when choosing a script for production. They will accomplish most when given a play in which the characters are three-dimensional, many-sided, and complex, rather than flat sterotypes. The script should provide the actor with enough information upon which to build a characterization, and at the same time, allow him enough latitude to stimulate his creative imagination. There should be enough depth and complexity in each role to hold the actors' interest throughout the rehearsal period. Each time they read the lines, if the characters are well-drawn, they will find in them some added connotations. Finally, the playwright should provide enough variety of mood within each role to challenge the actors' range of interpretative and emotional talents. A show that fails to excite the actors playing it cannot possibly communicate the author's purpose to the audience.

For example, the role of Olivia in *Night Must Fall* might appear at first reading to be almost a straight role. Rereading and rehearsal, however, will reveal Olivia to be an intense, sensitive, emotional, restrained, disappointed, intellectual woman. As she develops these qualities, all suggested in the script, the entire play will gain strengthened motivation, heightened emotional impact, and intensified suspense. Although Danny is the leading character, Olivia, Mrs. Bramson, Dora, and Mrs. Terence are all well-written roles, whose interpretation provides a stimulating exercise for student actors. Plays selected for high school production should provide several good roles, so that many students may become equally interested in and equally important to the presentation of the play. Plays written around a single good role and designed as star vehicles seldom make good material for secondary school productions.

Audience Requirements

Because the taste, or lack of it, of audience is usually the excuse given by high school directors who choose inferior plays for production, it seems important to analyze the demands that the audience make upon the play. To begin with, even audiences composed of high school students are not made up exclusively of village idiots, as one might assume by the fare so frequently selected "for them." It would be wise for directors engaged in educational theatre to assume, first, that the audience members are of average intelligence, and second, that they will accept a play that respects their intelligence more readily than one that insults it!

The auditor has a right to expect that a play contain enough physical action and visual interest that he can better understand the story by seeing and hearing it, than he could be reading it. Unless the material is poorly chosen, there is no substitute for being a part of a living audience watching living actors on a stage. One can only respect, not censure, the person who would rather curl up with a *good* book than go out to see a *poor* play.

The auditor may also expect to take something with him when he leaves the theatre. Therefore, the play should either inform, entertain, or provoke thought. Even, or perhaps especially, in high school productions, the auditor should never be able to walk out, shrug his shoulders, and say, "So what?"

This will surely be his reaction if two and a half hours of his time have been spent watching one of those unspeakable "written especially for high school" plays. The characters are mother, father, teen-age daughter, son, aged twelve, two teen-aged girl friends, one football hero, and two other big men on the campus. The theme is that every girl should go to the prom with a halfback; the big question is which formal to wear; and the complication is that little brother hides behind the sofa during the tender love scene and recites it to his parents at breakfast. It is good for a lot of laughing *at* the actors making fools of themselves. Such a play will insult the intelligence of the student as well as the adult members of the audience. In this era of world crisis, high school students are concerned with more important things than the junior prom, and they demand more meaningful subject matter in the plays produced by and for them. They know that they will be tomorrow's soldiers, parents, secretaries, merchants, teachers, doctors, nurses, and statesmen, and they would like to have a glimpse of their tomorrows on their stage!

Special Limitations in High School Play Selection

In addition to the requirements of the director, actors, and audience, play selection for high school must be limited by certain factors peculiar to production at this level. These are the limitations of physical equipment, actors' capacities, good taste, and budget allotment.

Physical Limitations

The teacher-director who has been trained in a well-equipped college or university theatre is apt to be discouraged by the facilities available to him in most high schools. High school auditoriums seem to be designed with band concerts and graduation exercises in mind, or perhaps with nothing whatever in mind. Like army uniforms, school stages seem to come in only two sizes—too large and too small. In these days of large city high schools, and consolidated rural high schools, the oversized stage is the more common. A proscenium opening, sixty feet wide and thirty-five feet high, certainly increases the problems of lighting, setting, and blocking of action for more or less awkward adolescent actors. A false proscenium, about thirty by twenty feet, placed just behind the front curtain would simplify the problems of setting, lighting, and staging. It can be achieved either by using draperies or teasers or by building a frame covered with wallboard or canvas and painted black. Sufficient ingenuity on the part of the director can compensate for any inadequacies in the physical stage. If it is small, he should not overlook the possibilities of extending the playing area out onto the apron or even into the orchestra pit.

The choice of a play may be somewhat limited by the number and type of lights available, by the equipment on hand, or by the trained technical crew. None of these obstacles, however, should stop the inventive director from doing the play he wishes to do. For his purposes, settings may be greatly simplified and yet remain highly effective. Unit sets, screens, silhouettes, set pieces, and a cyclorama are all devices that may be used to simplify settings. It is far better to use one of these techniques than to eliminate from the production schedule a play that is otherwise desirable. In addition, it should be noted than an exact reproduction of an elaborate Broadway set is usually a mistake, because it dwarfs the high school actors.

Actor Limitations

The choice of plays must always be affected by the number, sex, physical maturity, talent and training of the student actors available at any given time. However, there are few, if any, plays that cannot at *some* time be cast in a high school. The limitations of student actors must be considered only in terms of the current crop of talent. If one waits a few years, even a potential Hamlet or Lear will come along!

In selecting plays for high school actors, the director must consider certain conditions that usually prevail. There are nearly always more girls than boys among the budding Thespians; conversely, most plays contain more male than female roles. Some day a talented playwright with a practical turn of mind may make a fortune writing a few good plays with, let us say, ten women and five men in each cast. Until that time, directors must continue to beat the bushes for boys who can and will learn to act, and search the libraries for plays that don't require too many male performers.

Contrary to popular opinion, drama is easier for inexperienced actors than comedy. Most directors will agree that the sense of timing required in comedy and farce seems to be an inborn talent that is difficult, if not impossible, to teach. Just as some people are never able to tell a joke well, some are never able to deliver a humorous line in a play so that the audience will laugh. If talented comedians aren't available when it seems wise to select a show with high entertainment value, a mystery or modern melodrama is a good substitute. This type of show has the same escape value for the audience, and is easier to mold into a good production if there is doubt about the student actor's abilities.

Character roles are usually easier than straight ones for adolescent actors because they lose their self-consciousness when their own personalities are submerged in a character role. This does not mean that the director must select only shows like *The Silver Whistle* and *Old Lady Thirty-One,* but rather that he need not be confined to plays with predominantly juvenile characters. As a matter of fact, teen-aged actors have more difficulty portraying teen-aged characters than any other roles. They are so close to the roles in such plays as *Junior Miss* and *Time Out for Ginger* that they fail to see the humor in these characters. An actor must have both empathy with and an objective view of a character he is to play. Few adolescents can develop a balance between empathy and distance concerning comedy characters of their own age, although they can often achieve it with serious characters. High school actors generally can offer more convincing characterizations in plays that require historic costumes than in those done in modern dress. Perhaps disguising themselves also helps them to overcome self-consciousness. The high school director may, therefore, select plays with characters of all ages, and he might be wise to do as many period plays as possible.

Given skilled direction, high school students will turn in performances that compare favorably with those seen in college, community, and even professional theatre.

Good Taste Limitations

Probably the only serious problem in selecting plays for high school lies in what the community and school administrators consider to be in good taste for school presentation. Restrictions imposed by school boards, concerned parents, or immature student audiences may eliminate some fine plays that would otherwise be ideal for educational theatre. *The Happy Time,* for example, presents a delightful, healthy attitude toward the sexual curiosity and education of a teen-aged boy, but the situations and dialogue in it could be distorted by an audience of high school students who are trying to cover the embarrassment that their identification with the boy creates. Likewise, the ideas concerning responsible citizenship and corruption in politics in *Born Yesterday* are worth showing to a high school audience, but some school administrators or some parents might frown upon the presentation of Billie's openly living as Brock's mistress.

It is most unlikely that teen-agers will be more apt to become alcoholics because they see someone drinking tea from a cocktail glass on stage and calling it whiskey, but it might be wise for the director to avoid drinking whenever possible in his plays. A teacher-director who is new to his school and community may be well-advised to clear essential drinking scenes, like the one in *The Male Animal,* with the principal before producing the play.

Those young directors who, quite naturally, rebel against censorship in any form because it seems to be an abridgment of freedom of expression, would do well to analyze the objectives of their high school productions. These productions should be designed to bring to the student audience the ideas and intent of good plays that have educational values. In order to do this, it is important that the mood required by the script be maintained and that the illusion remain unbroken. Anything, therefore, that would provoke a response which would change the meaning or break the mood must be avoided. Adolescents at a school play, among their peers, do not react as they would as members of an adult audience. They remain self-conscious individuals rather than becoming members of the mass. Therefore, anything they see on the high school stage that is contrary to accepted public behavior for their age group might cause them to giggle self-consciously, and thus destroy the desired mood of the play. Passionate love scenes, profanity, drunkenness, and vulgar language can seldom be handled naturally and casually by either actors or audiences in the high school, because they are not acceptable campus behavior. Often the author's ideas may be more accurately and faithfully communicated by making some minor changes in the script than by offering it verbatim to the student audience.

British playwrights, for example, use the adjective "queer" repeatedly. American high school students understand this word only in the slang sense of "homosexual" so that the word "queer" must be replaced by "odd," "unique," "strange," "unusual," or some other innocent synonym, even in Barrie or Shaw. Similarly, the word "virgin" may call forth a dirty laugh from teenagers, but the word "chaste" probably would not. In a high school production of The Crucible, the word "strumpet" or "harlot" may be substituted for "whore" and the possibility of an inappropriate student audience response will be obviated. Teachers should be aware of the maturity of their students and take this factor into consideration. If teachers are aware of terms in the play that the students may misinterpret, it would be wise for them to discuss these terms with the students before attending the play. Sometimes all the students need is a word of warning to assure mature, appreciate reactions, rather than embarrassed giggles.

In some cases, the physical setting of a scene can cause difficulties with student audience behavior. Scenes played in a bedroom or on a bed may gain connotations before a high school audience which the author of the play never intended or even expected. Romeo's farewell to Juliet after their marriage and his banishment might be portrayed more effectively for an immature audience on the balcony than on the bed in Juliet's chamber. Similar changes of setting could eliminate embarrassment for the audience, and could still keep the mood of the play. If the teacher-director adjusts his own script and interpretation so that they will gain the proper audience response, it will not be necessary for an administrator to blue pencil the director's material.

The criteria for good taste may vary widely from one community to another, and may change rapidly from year to year. The director must be sensitive to these differences and willing to redefine his criteria for selecting and cutting plays. Judicious cutting, in most cases, can meet the requirements of good taste in plays that are otherwise suitable and desirable for school production.

The questions which the director must answer in regard to limitations of good taste are these:

Has the play enough positive educational value to justify its production?

Can necessary cuts be made without destroying the original intent?

If these answers are both affirmative, he should do the play.

Budget Limitations

Unlike commercial and community theatres, the budget for high school productions is probably the least troublesome of the limitations imposed upon play selection. If the show is at all acceptable, an audience of students and parents is assured in advance. It is nevertheless wise to consider the expenses involved, so that the school's drama program may at least be self-supporting, and perhaps make enough profit to help pay for the losses often incurred by athletics, band, dances, and other school activities.

The income from the box office should easily exceed the cost of production. Charging a nominal admission (tax-free) of one dollar per person, most high schools may expect to sell from $500.00 to $1,000.00 worth of tickets. Since there is no fee for rental of the theatre and there are no salaries to actors, director, or crews charged to the production, this amount is a generous one for other production costs. Items to be considered in the budget are royalty, scenery, printing, costumes, and furnishings. How much each of these costs will be, of course, depends upon the selection of the play.

The high school director will be wise to tear the "Non-Royalty" section out of his play catalogues and remember that in play royalties, as in most other things, he gets what he pays for. For no royalty, he may expect no show worth doing except in those plays now in public domain.[1] On standard shows, the budget should include royalty of twenty-five to fifty dollars for a single performance and fifteen to twenty-five dollars for each additional performance. Either by coincidence or design, costume shows usually have lower royalties than plays that require modern dress, so one cost often counterbalances the other.

[1] Copyrights can protect material for fifty-six years, after which it becomes public property and may be used without payment of royalty fees.

If the show is expensive to costume, the director will want to try to keep the cost of scenery and other items as low as possible. *Lady Precious Stream,* for example, requires rather elaborate costumes, but has no scenery and a relatively low royalty, so that the over-all cost of production can be kept within the budget limitations.

If there are the usual flats, doors, windows, and fireplaces on hand, the cost of repainting and remodeling these for each play is nominal. It certainly can be well done for less than fifty dollars for a one-set show. Here, again, the director must keep an eye on the budget, and avoid selecting a multiple-set play that is also expensive to costume.

Except for plays that require period furniture, it is usually quite easy to borrow furniture either from individuals in the community or from the local furniture stores. And the director who has not sat on boxes for a week while his living room furniture appears in his play is indeed a novice! In spite of the advice of Polonius, the director is apt to be both a borrower and a lender before he gets his show on the boards.

One hundred dollars will usually cover the cost of printing tickets and posters, although a considerable sum may be trimmed from this by having students make posters using a silk screen process. Programs may cost an additional fifty dollars, but this cost can also be reduced. Attractive programs can be mimeographed on colored paper at the school, or program advertising may be sold to local merchants to cover the cost of printing.

In addition to the noble causes of band and football uniforms, some part of the profits from high school plays should be set aside for purchasing additional equipment for the theatre: lights, drops, drapes, floor coverings, sound equipment, and so on. Some directors who cannot get this equipment fund from the profits of their shows have managed to obtain the needed items by adding them to the production budget of a particular show. "I can't possibly do *Our Town* without two more baby spotlights!" This technique may seem to be a little underhanded, but what good are thirty football helmets or two snare drums to the drama department?

Long Range Play Selection

Having developed an awareness of the requirements of director, actors, and audience, and of the limitations of physical equipment, student abilities, good taste, and budget, the director should strive for variety in the plays he selects, so that over a period of three or four years, many kinds of plays are offered to each generation of students at his school. Deciding which six or eight plays should be presented to students during their years in high school is something like trying to decide which books you would take with you if you knew you were to be cast upon a desert island. For all practical purposes, the high school is the desert island whereon its students may be exposed to theatre. The teacher-director is charged with the responsibility of selecting the only plays that students will see during their high school careers.

Every high school student should be exposed to a cross-section of drama in the theatre, as well as in the textbooks of English classes. He should see plays of different historical periods, different countries, different styles, and different themes. Perhaps this idea can be illustrated by discussion of a typical three-year "season" of plays directed by the author at Canoga Park High School: *Beggar on Horseback, Hamlet, She Stoops to Conquer, Look Homeward Angel, Little Mary Sunshine,* and *The Skin of Our Teeth.*

Beggar on Horseback is a comedy-fantasy about a struggling young musician and his temptation to marry a wealthy girl, so that he can spend his time composing, rather than giving lessons and copying music in order to exist. It contains elements of satire that broaden into farce and lend themselves, during the dream sequences, to expressionistic setting, costumes, and action.

FIGURE 26 *Beggar on Horseback*

Hamlet hardly requires justification for inclusion in the audience experience of high school students. The production of Shakespearean plays by and for high school students will be discussed in detail in a later chapter. It is sufficient to say here that, first, a play as difficult as *Hamlet* can only be selected when unusually talented student actors are available, and second, that Shakespeare must be seen on the stage by young people if they are to understand and appreciate his greatness as a playwright.

Seldom do the reading experiences in an English class contribute to this appreciation!

FIGURE 27   *Hamlet*

The eighteenth-century comedy of manners, *She Stoops to Conquer,* affords students an introduction to one of the most ornate, colorful, and robust periods in theatrical history. The perspective scenery, elaborate costumes, and stylized acting enhance the artificialty of the plot and characters. *She Stoops to Conquer* gives the student audience a better

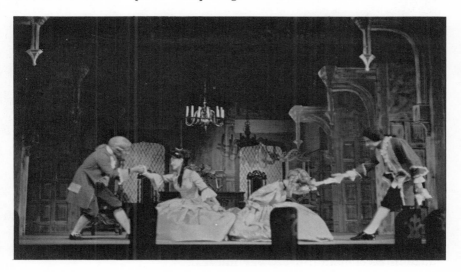

FIGURE 28   *She Stoops to Conquer*

understanding of the society of the period and an appreciation of the humor that evolves from language as well as from action.

Look Homeward Angel, the dramatization of Thomas Wolfe's autobiographical novel, is a play with which students readily identify. Eugene's problems of finding his own identity, understanding life, and becoming independent of his family are the same problems that students in the audience are currently experiencing. They empathize with Eugene, but they also gain insights into the problems of his parents, as they see the conflict between Gant's dreams of beauty and Eliza's practical approach to maintaining her family. Through *Look Homeward Angel,* perhaps students will see that both Gant and Eliza have dignity and value as human beings and that each makes the compromises necessitated by their joint responsibility for the family. They see that the parents do what they must do, just as Eugene does what he must do.

FIGURE 29   *Look Homeward Angel*

Pure entertainment was the chief reason for the selection of *Little Mary Sunshine,* which spoofs the obvious, melodramatic plots and stereotyped characters of the operettas of Romberg, Friml, and Herbert. Its songs are parodies of those of the operettas, and it has a relatively simple score, which can be done with piano rather than a complete orchestra. The sets are few and can be simplified to make it less expensive to stage than most musicals. Furthermore, *Little Mary Sunshine* can be done with actors rather than trained singers and does not involve the prolonged disruption of the entire high school, which often charatcerizes the production of elaborate Broadway musicals.

FIGURE 30   *Little Mary Sunshine*

Thornton Wilder's *The Skin of Our Teeth* completed this three-year "season" and gave the audience an experience with yet another kind of play. This comedy-drama, which encompasses the significant events in the history of Western civilization, is rich in allusions and philosophy that make it particularly appropriate for educational theatre. The use of period costumes for the refugees in the first act and simplification of the settings were the only changes made in *The Skin of Our Teeth*.

FIGURE 31   *The Skin of Our Teeth*

These six plays offer a wide range of theatre. The types include farce, tragedy, comedy of manners, and comedy-drama. The styles range from fantasy to romanticism, to satire, to realism. Nearly all are costume shows of different periods. The predominance of costume shows serves not only the actors, for reasons mentioned earlier in this chapter, but also the audience. The visual elements of a play are important in creating and sustaining audience interest. These six plays offer visual variety in their costumes and settings, as the production photographs on the preceding pages illustrate. Each has more than one set, and several have the elements of a spectacle, in movement as well as in setting and costume. So much diversity of subject matter and theme is found in these plays that it is impossible to summarize in a brief statement. If this season of six plays does not constitute a perfect introduction to the art of the theatre for a high school audience, it is at least a respectable attempt to offer plays of established quality, within the limitations of the production situation.

The limitations of play selection for high school production are not as restrictive as they may initially appear to be. They seem unimportant when the director's attention is focused upon introducing a student audience to the theatre. The director with vision and a wide knowledge of dramatic literature will find many plays that will stimulate him and his students to the highest level of achievement of which they are capable and will provide his audiences with experiences in theatre that constitute a genuine and lasting contribution to their education.

CHAPTER 14

Shakespeare on the High School Stage

Who is the greatest dramatist of all time? William Shakespeare, of course. Everyone knows that. Since Shakespeare is the greatest playwright the world has known, his plays should be produced by and for high school students. No student can pass through the school system without knowing that Shakespeare is supposed to be the world's greatest dramatist, yet very few students are convinced that this is true. In fact, most students do not like Shakespeare's plays, because they have encountered them in an English classroom rather than in a theatre. Shakespeare belongs in the theatre, and high school students should have an opportunity to meet him there.

Most educators would agree that students should see Shakespeare produced, but would wonder whether a high school could produce a play by Shakespeare well enough to serve any worthy purpose. The answer is yes. Although there are some special problems in producing Shakespeare, high schools can often present his plays well enough that the heterogeneous student audience can enjoy them and begin to understand why Shakespeare is a great playwright.

Cutting Shakespeare's Plays

Few directors would want to present an uncut version of a Shakespearean play, because the playing time might be as long as four or five hours. Thus, the primary reason for cutting is length. The director who does not feel capable of cutting a Shakespearean play may be able to find a published cut version that will satisfy him. I have been unable to find cut versions of Shakespeare that suited my tastes and needs. Some are too short, others omit sections that seem essential to a presentation without distortion, and still others cut lines that seem particularly beautiful. The best solution seems to be to make one's own cutting.

A director will usually wish to make some cuts for reasons other than length. The number of characters, especially male characters, in Shakespeare's plays creates casting problems in most high schools. Many minor roles can be eliminated, and others can be combined. Romeo need not have five friends to cheer him on in his encounter with Tybalt, and even though hosts of soldiers or courtiers add to the pageantry of Shakespeare's plays, their numbers can be reduced without weakening the plays. Other cuts may be made to assist the actors in making Shakespeare's ideas clear to modern audiences. There are often several lines of nonrestrictive phrases or clauses inserted between the subject and predicate in Shakespeare's sentences. The interpretation of these elaborate sentences is so difficult that the action of a scene may often be best implemented by omitting some embellishing phrases.

The task of cutting a Shakespearean play is both difficult and rewarding for the director. He will discover that Shakespeare's plays are much more tightly written than they appear to be at first. He will almost certainly begin by trying to cut out entire scenes, which seem to be nonessential, only to discover that each of them contains some vital plot lines, which cannot be omitted without changing the play's meaning or confusing the story. Whenever he cuts a scene, he will have to insert these plot lines elsewhere. Likewise, when he eliminates a minor character, the director will usually have to assign some of his lines to another character for the play to make sense. By the time the director has completed his cutting, he will know the Shakespearean play far better than he has ever known any other play, and consequently, he may surpass his usual quality of production when he stages it.

Staging Shakespeare

The settings for Shakespeare's plays may be either the most difficult or the simplest aspect of the production. They may be staged with no setting whatsoever, or on a replica of the Elizabethan stage, or with scenery designed to suggest the locale of each scene. Regardless of what style of setting is selected, the director and designer must bear in mind the nature of Shakespeare's plays and theatre. To the playwright, a change of locale did not mean a change of scenery; it meant only the movement of actors to a different area of the stage. Unless the settings designed for a production of Shakespeare permit a similar rapid flow of action, there is danger of frequent interruptions, which break the continuity and mood of the play. If the set changes take more than a few seconds, the effect is much like that of the late, late show on television, in which each ten minutes of the movie alternates with five minutes of commercials. The use of scenery can certainly help the audience to understand the environment of the play, if it is not allowed to become cumbersome.

By far the most difficult problem in the production of Shakespeare in a high school, or anywhere else, lies in the interpretation of the lines. It is here that Shakespeare's plays differ most from those of contemporary playwrights. The ability of the actors to read the lines meaningfully determines the success or failure of the production. When working with modern plays, the director and actors concern themselves with the emotional connotations of the lines of each character. They analyze the "why" and the "how" of the dialogue, in order to develop an accurate interpretation of the play. In modern plays, little or no time need be given to analysis of the "what" of the dialogue, because the "what" is usually obvious. In Shakespeare's plays, however, actors and director must concentrate first and continually upon what is being said. Only after they have completely understood the "what" of the lines can they begin to consider the "why" and the "how" according to the motivations of individual characters. It is part of the proof of Shakespeare's genius that the "what" is so specific, so detailed, that if it is completely understood the "why" and the "how" are obvious. The importance of knowing exactly what is said can be illustrated by a line from the famous, and too often satirized, balcony scene in *Romeo and Juliet*.

"O, Romeo, Romeo, wherefore art thou Romeo?"

More often than not, perhaps because Juliet delivers this line from her balcony at night before Romeo has revealed his presence to her, this line is read, or misread, as if it meant, "Romeo, where are you?" Once the actress understands that "wherefore" means "why" or "for what reason" rather than "in what place," she will read the line correctly. Not, "Romeo, Romeo, wherefore *art* thou, Romeo?" but, "Romeo, Romeo, *wherefore* art thou Romeo?" Not, "Where are you, Romeo?" but, "Why are you Romeo?" The correct reading of this line will also prevent the untimely laugh it gets when it is misunderstood and misread by the actress. How can the audience refrain from laughing when it sees Romeo under the balcony playing hide-and-seek while Juliet asks where he is?

The individual actor should be responsible for discovering the exact meaning of each line he has to speak, because an actor can only communicate to an audience what he understands himself. Of course, the director must be ready and able to assist when the actor has exhausted all his sources of information. What are the actor's sources? First, a thorough and repeated reading of the entire play. Second, a dictionary. Third, the annotations in a standard edition of the play. Fourth, a glossary of Elizabethan language. Fifth, himself—his logic, his instinct, his emotions. If the high school teacher-director and his actors apply themselves diligently to the task of interpreting the play, and devote a slightly longer period of time to its rehearsals, they will be able to present creditable productions of Shakespeare's plays. They will find their work with Shakespeare stimulating and satisfying.

High school directors who feel timid about attempting to produce Shakespeare's plays will find encouragement and guidance in Margaret Webster's *Shakespeare Without Tears*.[1] Miss Webster, who has directed many noteworthy productions of Shakespeare including several in which Maurice Evans starred, approaches Shakespeare as a practical craftsman of the living theatre and puts Shakespearean scholarship in its proper perspective.

In deciding which of Shakespeare's plays to produce, the teacher-director must apply the same criteria he uses in the selection of other plays. Some judgments about these plays are easier to make because they have already been tested by time. The most popular of Shakespeare's plays are doubtless those that communicate best to all audiences—*Hamlet, Romeo and Juliet, Othello, King Lear, Macbeth, Taming of the Shrew, As You Like It, Twelfth Night, Much Ado About Nothing,* and *The Merchant of Venice,* for example. American audiences probably do not have enough background in British history to be interested in Shakespeare's histories, but most of his tragedies and many of his comedies can and do appeal to audiences of American high school students.

Evaluating High School Shakespeare

Student reactions and responses to the productions of Shakespeare's plays are of paramount importance in evaluating their place in the high school's production schedule. Among the dozens of plays I have directed for high school, *Romeo and Juliet* and *Hamlet* have been the most popular with the students in the audience and in the casts. The student response to these plays may be significant.

The following incident provides the strongest testimonial to Shakespeare's greatness in this author's experience. After the first performance of *Romeo and Juliet* at Canoga Park High School, the head counselor asked me to come to her office. Her first words were "Now I see what you've been talking about all this time—about the importance of the arts to every kind of person and the need of every student for cultural experiences." The counselor told of a student, who had come to her office to report having seen *Romeo and Juliet*. The girl was nineteen years old and a Mexican-American. A Benet test showed an I.Q. of seventy-two,

---

1 Margaret Webster, *Shakespeare Without Tears* (New York: Fawcett World Library, 1942). Paperback.

and her composite score on the Iowa Test of Educational Achievement was in the third percentile. The student worked hard at her studies, and was about to graduate after four years in a three-year high school. She began by saying, "The most wonderful thing that ever happened to me in my life was seeing that play. It was so beautiful!" I am told the girl was crying as she spoke. The counselor naturally wondered whether this girl understood what she had seen, and asked her what the play was about. The girl then told the story in great detail. She had not read or seen the play before, yet she was able to understand all of it and even quote—almost exactly—many lines. The counselor recorded many of the girl's remarks. Here are some of them:

> The story was so beautiful. The setting was beautiful and the acting wonderful. It was a beautiful story of a teenage romance like today. They want to be in love and parents won't allow it. "Romeo, Romeo, Why art thou Romeo? Why art thou named Romeo?—Why hast thou died of my love, my sweet Juliet? My sweet Juliet, my sweet Juliet, you lie there so cold. I shall kiss thy lips remembering thee,—I shall take the poison so I can be with thee in peace!" So beautiful, I'd love to see it over and over— it was so beautifully done.

(Of course, we let her come to another performance. Who could resist such an audience!) The girl went on to say, "I love the plays we see here at school. Next to this one, the one I liked best and thought was beautiful was *Medea*. I saw it in the tenth grade."

It is impossible to explain this girl's reaction. I can't. It is interesting that in between *Medea* and *Romeo and Juliet,* she saw *Time Out for Ginger, The Glass Menagerie, Jenny Kissed Me, The Matchmaker,* and *The Madwoman of Chaillot.* I think she showed remarkable taste in preferring *Medea* and *Romeo and Juliet* to the others. Maybe that is why the classics are the classics.

Other students showed their approval of this production by coming to see it a second time. Approximately four hundred students bought tickets and saw *Romeo and Juliet* twice. As a rule, only a handful of students come to see plays again

Playing Shakespeare's roles is the most valuable experience an actor can have. In one sense, the roles he has written are easier to play than those of lesser playwrights. Shakespeare gives the actor more beautiful language to speak and much more specific information upon which to build his character than other writers. Students who had appeared in *Hamlet* made the following observations when asked to compare the experience with that of acting in other plays!

The boy who played *Hamlet* said, "Shakespeare is more fun, more rewarding, because of the beauty of the language. The words sound like the emotions. Other plays seem shallow after doing Shakespeare."

Other students offered these ideas. "Shakespeare is not a realist. His characters free your imagination. The individual actor *must* understand the character or he can't play it. You keep learning more about your character every time you rehearse."

"The tone and mood is understandable even if you do not understand all the words. For example, '. . . the morn, in russet mantle clad, walks o'er the dew of yon high eastward hill.' That's so beautiful you can just see and feel the dawn!"

"I'd go to see the same play by Shakespeare over and over if I could. I don't think I'd ever get tired of it because I find something new—something more—each time. I never got bored with rehearsals. Most plays I'm sick of by the time we get them on."

What these students were saying is that Shakespeare's plays are inexhaustible. Like all great works of art, Shakespeare's plays can never be totally comprehended. One never tires of great art because it is inexhaustible. How long, how often can you look at a Rembrandt? How many times can you hear Hamlet muse, "To be or not to be, that is the question. Whether it is nobler in the mind to suffer the slings and arrows of outrageous fortune, or to take arms against a sea of troubles and by opposing end them. . . ."

There is no doubt that meeting Shakespeare in the theatre was a valuable educational event for all these students. High school directors should produce Shakespearean plays regularly.

Directors and actors should attempt to interpret Shakespeare but not to improve upon his work. The current fad among theatrical directors of attempting to prove their creativity by doing something new, or original, or different with Shakespeare is a disservice to the playwright, the director, and the audience. Most productions that change the period or locale of Shakespeare's plays are less successful than traditional interpretations. Modern dress productions often create confusion in the minds of any audience. A modern Juliet, for example, would not be apt to have a nurse. A tuxedo-clad Hamlet and Laertes engaging in a duel with poison-tipped swords is a bit incongruous!

The continuing appeal of Shakespeare lies not in the details of plot and props but rather in the universality of his characters, themes, and emotions and in the beauty of his poetic use of language. These elements become more timely, more immediate for a modern audience if the plays are costumed in the period of their action rather than in modern dress. When seen in period costumes, the universality of Shakespeare's plays is strikingly revealed, as the modern audience empathizes with the characters without breaking the aesthetic distance.

Ben Jonson's comment that Shakespeare was not of an age, but of all time, has been reconfirmed by the increasing number of Shakespearean productions in the past decade. Student reaction to Shakespeare in high school suggests that Shakespeare is not for an age, but for all ages—including the teens.

CHAPTER 15

Play Reading, Viewing, and Analysis

Because all the theatrical arts except that of playwrighting are ephemeral, plays are the most vital and fundamental part of any high school course in drama. As much reading, both individual and group, and as much attendance of plays as possible, followed by study and analysis of these experiences, should be required of every drama student regardless of his previous background or his specialized interests.

Purposes of Play Reading, Viewing, and Analysis

A high school can seldom produce more than one full-length play each semester, and many of the great plays can never be produced by high schools, as pointed out in the preceding chapter, because of the limitations of maturity of the students, of physical facilities, of budget, and of good taste. Since the primary value of drama in general education rests upon dramatic literature, a method must be found to acquaint students with at least some of this literature.

For the few students whose interest in theatre is more than an avocational, recreational one, the study of plays will provide the best possible background for their future training in any of the specialized areas of the theatre arts. Just as the composer, conductor, or soloist will be more sensitive and creative if he has a broad background knowledge of musical literature, so the playwright, director, or actor will do a better job if he has a broad knowledge of dramatic literature. Therefore, the study of plays will serve the diversified needs of all students in the drama class. To expand the cultural and aesthetic experiences of the general student, as well as to lay the foundation for the specialized student of theatre, the teacher should require all students to analyze, orally or in writing, significant plays they have read or seen in the theatre, motion pictures, or television.

Oral Reports

Oral reports, presented to the entire class, about important plays of various nations, historical periods, and strata of society seem to be an ideal method of giving the students some knowledge of the scope, evolution, universality, and pervasiveness of drama in civilization. To afford students a survey of dramatic literature, a list of major periods and plays similar to the following may be used.

> Greek: *Oedipus Rex* or *Medea*
> Middle Ages: *Everyman* or *Master Pierre Patelin*
> Elizabethan: *Romeo and Juliet* or *The Taming of the Shrew*
> Seventeenth Century: *Tartuffe* or *The Doctor In Spite of Himself*
> Eighteenth Century: *The School for Scandal* or *She Stoops To Conquer*
> Nineteenth Century: *An Enemy of the People* or *A Doll's House*
> Twentieth Century: *Death of a Salesman* or *The Skin of Our Teeth*

Two students may be assigned to each theatrical period and given a couple of weeks to prepare the report, which they will jointly present to the class. They may include in this report a biographical sketch of the playwright, historical background of the era and the play, and the plot and theme of the play. To further enliven the assignment and to prevent it from becoming another routine book report, they may also select an outstanding scene from the play and read it to the class, thereby illustrating the style of the playwright and the idiom of the particular period and locale. The presentation of each report, followed by class discussion, will probably take a full class period.

Written Reports

Each student's background in dramatic literature may be further broadened by the assignment of plays to be read for individual written reports and analysis. Before such assignments are made, however, some instruction in how to read a play should be given. Since plays lack the detailed descriptive passages found in the other forms of literature that students are accustomed to reading, and since a play is not complete until it is presented upon a stage before an audience, the reader of a play must compensate for the absence of actors, setting, and physical action. His visual and auditory imagination must supplement the skeleton script of the play.

The student should begin his reading of a play by carefully studying the description of the setting, consulting pictures, and floor plans, if such are available, until he has a clear mental picture of the set, decor, and placement of furnishings. Next, either before he begins to read the dialogue or as each new character is introduced, he should form a clear picture of each character in his imagination. He should cast the play in his mind so that each character will appear to him as he reads the dialogue. Skill in this reading technique will come with practice, and by the time he has read two or three plays, the absence of detailed description will seem an asset rather than a handicap to his reading.

So that they may better understand and appreciate the plays they are required to read, beginning drama students may be asked to write their reports according to the following outline.

    I. Identification
      A. Title
      B. Playwright
        1. Biographical data
        2. Other works
      C. Period of action
      D. Date of writing or first production
   II. Dramatic Analysis
      A. Type
      B. Style
      C. Kind of conflict
      D. Protagonist
      E. Antagonist
      F. Theme
  III. Plot Analysis
      A. Exposition
      B. Inciting incident
      C. Rising action
      D. Climax
      E. Conclusion
  IV. Essay of evaluation
   V. Breakdown of sub-plot (same as III)
  VI. Discussion of differences between Shakespearean and other plays.

At least once during the semester, students should be required to read a Shakespearean play. Steps V and VI should be included in this report. The chief difficulty for high school students in reading Shakespeare seems to be following the main plot line through all the subplots, incidental scenes, and long speeches. So that the uninitiated reader won't become discouraged halfway through the first act, he should study carefully a plot outline or summary before he begins to read any Shakespearean play. With the plot well in mind, he may read easily through the play and be free to enjoy the subtlety and wit of the dialogue, the depth of characterization, and the beauty of Shakespeare's language. To crystalize his impressions of the play, he may reread the plot outline after finishing the play and then proceed to write his report. There can be no more gratifying experience in teaching than to see a boy of sixteen grin with pride when he discovers that he can actually read, understand, and enjoy Shakespeare. He suddenly gains confidence in himself, and from that point on teaching him is pure joy!

It may be noted here that character descriptions are not included in this outline for beginning students' reports on play reading. The reasons for this are as follows: first, the beginning course is a general one often substituted for an English class; second, class discussions give sufficient emphasis to this phase of plays; third, most students (like all actors) tend to read only the roles with which they identify themselves rather than the entire play, and this tendency should be discouraged.

Some explanation of this outline must, of course, be given to the students. The general terms used are defined in almost any basic text in drama or literature. The outline can be best understood if the entire class can read the same play and analyze it together in class with the assistance of the teacher.

Usually the student finds his greatest difficulty in making a concise statement of the theme of a play. He finds it difficult to separate theme from plot and to express the theme in terms of a generality rather than a specific taken from the particular story. In order to teach the student to find a play's theme, it may be necessary to show him several examples of the difference between theme and plot. This may be done by discussion of plays recently produced at the school or by using recent television dramas with which the student is familiar as examples to show that the plot is used to illustrate or prove the playwright's theme. At first, plays whose themes are uncomplicated should be used, such as, *Dear Brutus,* "The fault . . . lies not in our stars, but in ourselves, that we are underlings"; *Death Takes A Holiday,* "Love is stronger than death"; *What Every Woman Knows,* "Behind every great man there is a great woman"; *You Can't Take It With You,* "Enjoy your life and wealth while you live, because you can't take it with you"; or *Summer and Smoke,* "Of all sad words of tongue or pen, the saddest are these: It might have been."

The steps of the plot may be illustrated by a pyramid diagram and briefly defined as follows:

EXPOSITION: The background information of time, locale, relationship of characters, and initial situation, which the reader must have in order to understand the story.

INCITING INCIDENT: The first piece of action that demands further development and initiates the major conflict.

RISING ACTION: The series of incidents that develop the conflict and further complicate it.

CLIMAX: The point of decision or point of no return at which the ultimate fate of the protagonist is decided.

FALLING ACTION: The incidents that give details of the resolution of the conflict and the fate of the other characters.

CONCLUSION: The final incident in the story.

If students can be convinced that there is no penalty for honest comment, even when it disagrees with the teacher's point of view, the fourth step in the outline can be the most valuable one for teaching. From the student's evaluation of the play he has read, the teacher may determine whether the student's taste and critical abilities are growing.

Those students who, because of their interests and ability, enter a second course in drama may be given a somewhat more challenging outline for their play reports.

   I. Title
  II. Playwright
      A. Biographical data
      B. Other works
 III. Theme, purpose, central idea
 IV. Mood
  V. Method
 VI. Total effect

The first three steps in this outline are identical to those the students have used in the beginning course in drama. The detailed breakdown of plot is omitted, because the students have already learned that plays have a systematic structure that is not accidental. That art has form is an important idea for beginning students to understand.

In step IV, mood, of the advanced outline, the student is asked to describe the emotional atmosphere of the play. He must decide what the predominant mood is and discuss where and by what means it is established by the playwright. Any changes of mood and the contribution these changes make to the dramatic impact of the play should also be included in this discussion. It is in this discussion that the student's emotional sensitivity is revealed.

In step V, method, the student should describe the playwright's technique and style. The student attempts to decide how the playwright develops his theme through plot, characterization, dialogue, and setting. It is here that the motivations of the major characters and their functions in the play are discussed. The major conflict and its resolution must also be defined in relation to the playwright's method.

Step VI, total effect, is designed to allow the reader to consider himself a member of an audience viewing the play and to evaluate the play's impact on an audience. Did the playwright achieve his purpose? Was the play interesting dramatic material? Does it have general audience appeal or is it directed toward a particular age group, era, strata of society, or nationality? All these, and many other questions, may be considered in determining the total effect—the retrospective view—of the play read.

Selection of Plays for Reading

Unless the teacher offers some definite guidance in the choice of plays to be read by students, these assignments and reports may be only "busy work," which contributes nothing constructive to the students' background in theatre. The scope and content of the drama class is so broad that there is no time to include any but the most meaningful assignments. To guide their selection of plays for reports, students should be given either a list of plays or a list of recommended playwrights. If the plays available in the school's library have been purchased with the assistance of the drama teacher, the teacher can possibly restrict the students' reading to those plays found in the library and thereby be assured of adequate limitations. A list of plays recommended for student reading appears in the appendix.

Although the individual student's interest, ability, and growth are the most important factors in guiding his program of play reading, some general policies may be suggested. First, the uninitiated reader of plays should start with works that are easy to understand, simple in structure, and high in emotional or entertainment values. Contemporary comedies and melodramas, by playwrights like George S. Kaufman, Moss Hart, Howard Lindsay, Russel Crouse, Emlyn Williams, Noel Coward, Agatha Christie, and James M. Barrie, might be recommended for the initial assignment in play reading. Greek tragedies are also easy for beginning students to analyze, because of the simplicity of their structure. The three unities, time, place, and action, make them easy to understand. The second assignment might be selected from slightly more complex plays by contemporary playwrights like Maxwell Anderson, Eugene O'Neill, Tennessee Williams, Clifford Odets, Thornton Wilder, or Arthur Miller. After this, the students might move to selections from plays by Henrik Ibsen, George Bernard Shaw, Ferenc Molnar, Karel Capek, August Strindberg, and Anton Chekhov. Finally, the student's play reading assignments may be taken from earlier playwrights like Molière, Goldsmith, Sheridan, Jonson, and Shakespeare.

It should perhaps be noted here that the limitations placed upon play selection for production in high school do not apply to the selection of plays for student reading.

Sources of Plays for Reading

The collections of plays in the school and public library may be supplemented by a relatively inexpensive classroom library of plays. Paperback editions of individual plays and anthologies, ranging in price from fifty cents to a dollar and a half, are readily available. The best plays of every playwright and every period can be obtained for a classroom library. This library can be financed by voluntary student memberships. Each student who joins pays fifty cents and has access to all the books purchased with his and his classmates' fees.

Evaluation of plays on a stage should also be an important part of each drama student's training. Theatre-going opportunities are usually available at college and community theatres, if professional theatre is not nearby, and all students can see plays on television. A television play, which all students are assigned to see, can be used to introduce analysis of productions, just as a play read in common is used to explain play analysis. Using this common experience of seeing a play, either in a theatre or on television, students can compare their reactions to the script, setting, acting, directing, and other aspects of the production. Students may then be assigned, individually, to see plays and television dramas and write critical essays about these experiences. Rather than being given a structured outline, they should be asked to read reviews in newspapers and magazines and use them as a guide to their own critiques.

Samples of Students' Reports

The following examples of student reports and reviews may serve to clarify these assignments. All are unedited, and all are written by students in the upper 10 percent of their classes. In the first report, the teacher's comments are included in parenthesis, as an illustration of the kind of corrections that will help the student improve the quality of his next report. It seems worthwhile, incidentally, to require each student to write all his reports in a spiral type notebook, so that he can refer to the teacher's comments on past assignments as he writes each new play report.

The following is a first play report by a tenth grade girl, aged fourteen.

I.   The play is *Summer and Smoke*.

II.   It was written by Tennessee Williams. He was born in Columbia, Mississippi in 1924. He grew up in the South, for the most part St. Louis. He attended Washington University in St. Louis, but left in his sophomore year. He returned to college in 1936 and acquired a degree at the University of Iowa. After his graduation he held odd jobs, during which time he wrote, mostly for the stage. In 1939 he won a small cash prize for four one-act plays. In 1940 he won a scholarship. His first success was *The Glass Menagerie*, 1945.

(Although many of his plays are good, I think that this is the only one, to date, which time may prove to be a great play. I hope you've read it.) Less successful was *You Touched Me*, 1946. In 1947, he had a huge success in *A Streetcar Named Desire*. *Summer and Smoke* failed on Broadway, but his next production *The Rose Tattoo*, 1949 was successful. Williams has also written a collection of one-act plays.

III.   *Summer and Smoke* was first presented by Margo Jones at her theatre in Dallas, Texas. It was presented in New York at the Music Box Theatre on October 6, 1948.

IV.   The play's central idea is the lamentably ironic story of two people's lives which cross frequently, yet somehow never actually touch, of two people who are never ready for each other at the same time. (Is there a general observation about society or people which is pointed up by this story? The theme is the principle or moral that the specific story illustrates. Can you state the central idea of this story in general terms of a truth about people that might apply to other situatons?)

V.   Exposition. One learns of the fact that young Alma Winemiller is a preacher's daughter and John Buchanan is the son of a doctor in the prologue. One also partially learns of their relationship. By seeing them as children, it is easier to understand them as adults. Scene one takes place, as did the prologue, in the park by the Fountain of Eternity. John and Alma are now adults. One gathers from the dialogue that John has been out of town with a floating crap game. Dr. Buchanan appears and John pretends not to see him. John hadn't notified his father of his return and apparently didn't wish to do so for some time. Their relationship is very strained. Dr. Buchanan has obviously been quite angry and upset over the way John is conducting his life, for some time. Alma appears with her parents. Alma describes the panic she felt while singing to the people at the band concert, she is going to wait for a fellow named Roger. Her father shows his unfavorable opinion of John by requesting she wait as far away from him as possible. The period of the play starts as summer during a year shortly before World War I. The place is Glorious Hill, Mississippi. The first step in the plot is when John throws a firecracker at Alma (pretending an imaginary little boy did it) in order to have a chance to talk to her.

Rising Action. He and Alma talk for awhile. His attention wanders from Alma to Rosa Gonzales, who has come into the plaza (his attention is easily diverted). As the play progresses, John becomes quite involved with Rosa and her way of life. This is a constant source of frustration for Alma as she is in love with him. At one point it seems that Alma has won John's affections, but it develops that their concepts of love are exactly opposite. Alma becomes insulted and angry and leaves accusing him of not being a gentleman. One night, the next winter, there is a wild party at John's, and Alma calls his father long distance. Dr. Buchanan returns and is shot by Rosa's father, who is quite drunk. This ends John's relationship with Rosa. But at the same time it doesn't endear Alma to him. He tells her he is sick of her preaching and affected poses and he wishes she would try acting like a human being. Even so he begins to admit to himself that he respects her. The next autumn, John, who has given up his wild life since his father's death and become a dependable doctor, meets Nellie Ewall. That winter Alma realizes John and Nellie will probably be married. Deep down inside Alma believes there is no hope for her and John. Yet she can't bring herself to just let her hopes go. The climax comes when she goes to John's office and tells him that she's changed her set of values and she now believes in his views on life. However, he has come around to her way of thinking. He now believes that there should be such things as respect. He tells her she was right about an argument they had had—people do have souls.

Falling Action. Nellie comes in. She tells Alma that she and John are to be married. Alma says she had guessed as much and she hopes they'll be happy. She leaves and goes to the park. The conclusion is when the new Alma (more natural and at ease) meets a young traveling salesman at the park and leaves with him for Moon Lake Casino (previously owned by Gonzales), not wanting to be left empty-handed.

VI. I enjoyed the play very much. I like it quite a bit better than *A Streetcar Named Desire.* I suppose this is because it was less brutal than *Streetcar.* There is something rather delicate and fragile about the play. I imagine this feeling exists mainly through Alma. I have a tendency to like a play, to the degree that I do, largely because of characters which I feel would or wouldn't be interesting and fascinating to play. And in my opinion, Alma Winemiller would certainly fulfill these conditions.

The next student report was written by a second semester drama student, an eleventh grade girl, aged sixteen, who was a college preparatory student. It was also the first assignment of this kind.

PLAY. *The Crucible*

AUTHOR. Arthur Miller. This new playwright has been acclaimed as the outstanding new dramatist of the 1940's, or at least as the equal of Tennessee Williams among new authors. Miller was born in New York, in 1916 and attended high school there, playing football and doing the typical things an American boy is said to do. He attended the University of Michigan, after earning money for a couple of years, and won laurels for his talents in writing. Upon leaving college in 1938, he was employed in the Federal Theatre writing project. Later he wrote for radio shows, etc., and his first play to score a success was *All My Sons* in 1947. Two years afterward, he had Broadway at his feet for *Death of a Salesman.* Brooks Atkinson called it "one of the finest dramas in the whole range of the American theatre." The play won the Pulitzer Prize as well as the Drama Critics' Circle Award. Four years later, Miller's most recent play opened, *The Crucible,* and it too is being hailed as a great play. Again, Brooks Atkinson of the New York Times says, "Arthur Miller has written another powerful play."

THEME: Man will persecute others because of selfish wants, or ignorance, or fear, and many will suffer who are innocent. Propaganda, dissatisfaction, and fear of the unknown may heighten those persecutions. That which is not true is much more easily believed, and the truth is much more difficult to prove than lies.

MOOD: Heavy, dramatic, tense. The play would be classified as a tragedy. It is historical also.

METHOD: To prove the theme, the author does not use present-day United States, communists, and Senator McCarthy, but sets the play in Salem, Massachusetts, in 1692. He chooses to tell about the famous Salem Witch Trials. The play is historically accurate. Only a few changes has he made. He raised the ages of the children involved in the accusing and diminished their number. He also reduced the number of judges.

It is difficult to write about the method of the play, since it is not just this author proving his theme, but actual historic facts. The story is told through plot and characters. Several of the characters undergo complete changes of opinion during the play, which heightens the horror of the epidemic, when you realize the witchburners are outwitting everybody. The play is written in four acts, and each act is one complete scene. Each act is complete and dynamic. The author used the language of the time, which is easily understood, but many of the constructions sound formal and strange. The accusations are all silly and based upon petty jealousies, or because the accused behaves in a way that is a little unconventional. Those who are not entirely conventional are persecuted. The desire of the children to be the center of attention is also a factor that led to the epidemic. To clinch the theme, John Proctor, the leading character, is hung in the end, rather than admit to a crime he did not commit. This proves his innocence.

EFFECT: The idea is stimulating, and the parallel drawn between the witch trials and our own situation is obvious. The over-all picture of the period as shown in this play is authentic and convincing. The reader or audience is left with a feeling of awe and anger at the curtain.

The final student report is a review of a professional play, and was written by a beginning drama student. It follows no assigned outline because, as mentioned, students are instructed to read professional critics and try to follow the pattern set in their reviews.

I Am A Camera, by John Van Druten

Mr. Van Druten's play is based on the Christopher Isherwood stories of Berlin. The play centers on the way of life of an amoral English girl, Sally Bowles (Julie Harris) as seen through the eyes of the camera, Isherwood (Charles Cooper). The time is 1930, before the rise of the Hitler regime. Caught in the Nazi rise and their own romance are Fritz Wendel (William Allyn) and Natalia Landauer (Janet Dowd). By the end of the play they have partially settled their future. However, at the end Sally has resolved nothing; she hasn't changed at all since the beginning of the play. As a matter of fact nothing has; nothing is decided; nothing is settled; nothing is accomplished.

It is my opinion, though not that of the New York drama critics, that Van Druten's play completely lacks merit. It is trivial and uninteresting.

I didn't so much mind the fact that there are loose ends left lying around at the end of the third act, as I did the fact that the play doesn't seem to have any sort of purpose. It does simply what the title implies—it records the constant flow of life. In doing this, it succeeds only in being extremely repetitious. Although I am usually critical of plays, I am not, as a rule, bored by them. However, there is a first time for everything and this was it. I don't ever recall looking forward with such eagerness to the third act curtain. I'm certain that had I had the opportunity to read the play before December I should never have wasted my time and money in going to see it.

Julie Harris was good, but I didn't find her brilliant. However, she did seem to have some sort of spark. There was one thing I definitely objected to—Miss Harris drew out her "s" to an unbelievable degree. I'm afraid I didn't judge her fairly as I disliked the play so thoroughly.

Charles Cooper gave a mediocre performance. His Chris never once came to life. It was all quite mechanical. But I will grant that it is rather difficult to play someone who is living and whom one has probably met.

William Allyn's performance was no better, but the faults were not the same. The most noticeable of his faults was his German accent, which was decidedly French. Though Mr. Allyn was not outstanding, he wasn't really bad.

Janet Dowd's performance was among the better ones. Her German accent was good and so was her characterization.

Alga Fabian was quite good in the role of Fraulein Schneider, and landlady. Her work seemed more inspired and less mechanical.

The role of a wealthy American tourist, Clive Mortimer, was played by Edward Andrews. Although he was amusing, he was never believable because he overdid.

Mrs. Watson-Courtneidge, Sally's mother, was portrayed by Harriet McGibbon. I have a sneaky hunch that her characterization came from a mold. Regardless of this, things seemed to pick up during her scenes.

Boris Aronson's setting did all it should; it neither detracted from the general effect nor got in the way. The cluttered room did quite a good job of supplying the proper atmosphere.

Ellen Goodsborough's costumes served their purpose. The only one of the costumes I objected to was worn by Julie Harris in the first and third acts. I felt it could have been more subtle without running the danger of not being understood.

John Van Druten directed his play. His direction was very capable. I'm sure he achieved everything with his play he wished and who should know what the author wants done with his work better than that man himself?

I wish I could say I liked *I Am A Camera*, but I can't help wondering what *the worst was like if that was the best.*

Effect of Play Reading and Analysis

Assignments of this nature—reading and seeing plays—are both interesting and challenging to students, once their initial resistance to anything that seems like "book work" in a drama class is overcome. Perhaps the first lesson to be learned in a high school drama class is that theatre consists of study, skill, and labor, not merely inspired play.

Once the techniques of play reading have been mastered, students learn to enjoy reading plays. Most read many more than the assigned number. Similarly, once they have had the thrilling experience of being a member of a theatre audience, students catch the fever and develop a theatre-going habit. Often, they continue to read reviews of plays and motion pictures and use them as guides to their attendance at theatres.

These assignments in reading and seeing plays open new avenues of cultural interest and aesthetic appreciation to the students, which they are likely to pursue the rest of their lives.

CHAPTER **16**

Directing and Producing the Play

The production of a *fully mounted,* full-length play in the high school is the culmination of the participants' studies in drama, stagecraft, and design, and the showcase in which they display their knowledge and talent. For the drama teacher-director, the production and direction of the play is the most difficult, important, and visible part of his job. In the production of each play, the director, like his students, displays his knowledge and talent. His success or failure as a drama teacher is judged almost entirely by the quality of the productions he directs. It is proper that he be judged by his productions, because they affect the education of every student in the school.

The high school teacher of drama must act as both producer and director (and sometimes technical director) of his shows, and must, therefore, organize every detail of the production so that he will have time to oversee the whole process.

Selection and Beginning

Criteria for play selection have been discussed in detail in Chapter 13, but it should be repeated here that the director must make the final decision about what play is to be produced, because he is best able to assess all the factors that will affect the production.

The play should be selected about ten weeks before the proposed opening date in order to allow ample time for planning all phases of the production. As soon as the play has been selected, permission to produce it, together with a royalty quotation, should be obtained from the publisher and copies of the script should be purchased. In requesting the royalty quotation, the director should inform the publisher of the number of performances, the anticipated size of audiences, and the price of admission. With this information to evaluate, publishers often quote a lower royalty fee than that listed in their catalogues. At least ten copies of the script beyond the number required by the cast should be ordered.

As soon as the scripts arrive, copies of the play should be distributed to the students in the play production class and to the teachers of stage design and stagecraft. The director must begin to study the script to decide on his interpretation of the play and to make any cuts or revisions that are required. As soon as these decisions are made, they should be transmitted to everyone concerned with the production.

In cooperation with the teachers of design and stagecraft, the director should decide on a floor plan for each set in the play. The director should also make a production and rehearsal schedule for all students, parents, faculty, and administrators concerned with the production of the play. A sample rehearsal and production schedule is reproduced in the Appendix C.

Casting

Casting may well be the most important responsibility of the director. A director who casts his show well may do almost nothing else and still produce a good show. On the other hand, a director may so handicap his production by errors in casting that nothing he nor anyone else does will make the show a success. Most theatrical directors could improve the quality of their shows by paying more careful attention to casting.

Several pitfalls in the casting process may trap the unwary or inexperienced director. The first of these is type-casting. Looks can indeed be deceiving when a director has too definite an idea about how each character must look. It is more important for Falstaff to have a sense of comedy than to be fat. Knowing that Anthony Perkins created the role they are trying to cast, some directors may cast the boy who looks most like Anthony Perkins. The director should try to keep an open mind about the physical requirements of the characters he is seeking to cast.

A smooth first reading can sometimes fool a director into miscasting an important role. A student with a good voice and an air of authority may be too impressive when compared to others who are very nervous at a first reading. Sometimes the student who hits upon the right characterization and interpretation in the first reading may do so by accident. He may not know what he did or be able to repeat it. He may also be what the theatrical profession calls a "radio actor," who gives everything he has in the reading but is unable to develop the role any further.

The dangers of precasting were mentioned in an earlier chapter. In addition to the fact that the director who precasts may overlook a better actor, he may also find that he cannot cast other roles in the play to match those he has precast. For example, a boy who is five feet, six inches tall, might be excellent as Romeo if Juliet is also short. The same Romeo would be ludicrous opposite a Juliet who is five feet, ten inches tall!

Perhaps the most tempting and dangerous casting pitfall for the director is the personality trap. How satisfying it would be to give the overbearing, egotistical, ill-mannered student a bit part or none at all. And wouldn't it be wonderful to be able to give a leading role to that helpful, hard-working, friendly student who has been gathering props and going out for your coffee for two years and deserves some recognition. Unfortunately, some very nice people cannot act and some very good actors are unpleasant people. The director who consistently produces shows of good quality is the one who is able to separate his personal feeling from his theatrical judgment when casting.

Casting well takes time—more time than most directors are willing to allow for it. Anxious to start rehearsals, directors rush through the casting process in a day or two when they should spend a week or two at this task. There are, however, some techniques for conducting tryouts that can save time. Students should have an opportunity to read the entire play and to prepare for the tryouts before reading for the director. The director should select and announce the sections of the play he plans to use in casting each character. It will be easier for the director to evaluate each actor's reading if these scenes are brief and include only one or two other characters. Time will be saved if the director announces which characters and scenes he wishes to read each day of tryouts. He should also explain to those who are trying out what he considers to be the most important requirements of each character.

Although each member of the class must be given the opportunity to read for every role that interests him, every actor cannot try every role at every tryout. As the tryouts progess, the director should narrow the field of those attempting each part to two or three actors. When he does this, he should tell those who are eliminated why he considers them unsuitable for the role.

What should the director try to observe as he conducts tryouts? Obviously, interpretation, phrasing, and characterization are important. Even in a reading, actors should listen, react, pause, think, and attempt to motivate the lines. Empathy is also important, and empathy is affected by both the vocal and the physical qualities of the player. In real life, overweight girls with buck teeth do fall in love, marry, and live happily ever after; but on the stage, Emily Webb must be physically attractive if a production of *Our Town* is to succeed. Although type-casting is not wise, the director must consider whether or not makeup and costume can make an actor look acceptable in his role. Vocal empathy is more often overlooked in casting than visual empathy. Again, in spite of the facts of real life, stage heroes do not have high-pitched voices, nor do sympathetic characters have strident ones. During tryouts, the director should spend a considerable amount of time with his eyes closed or his back to the readers to be sure that their voices as well as their appearances suit the characters.

In casting roles of any length, the director must look for variety—vocal and emotional variety—in the actor's reading. The actor who reads every line with the same vocal pattern and every scene with the same emotional intensity will soon lose the attention of an audience. Before key roles are cast, the director should ask those he is considering to read sections of the play that require different emotional attitudes. An actor may read Mr. Antrobus' second act campaign speech in *The Skin of Our Teeth* very effectively and be unable to play the third act, in which he is weary, then angry, and finally warmly philosophical.

Perhaps the most important quality the director must find in the actors who are to play major roles is flexibility. Can the actor take direction? Can he change his interpretation when the director gives him a different motivation? Can he understand the direction? Will he accept it? If the actors cannot take direction, it is impossible to develop a unified production that interprets the play as the director understands it. Regardless of how good an actor's reading may be, even if it is exactly what the director envisioned, the director should suggest a different approach to some part of the role in order to discover if the actor is flexible.

It has already been implied that the major roles, or the more difficult roles, should be cast first. A weak actor in a major part will ruin the show, but in a small part, he will only cause the audience a few moments of discomfort. However, before any casting is set, the director must consider the entire group of characters and their relationships to one another in the play. When his show is well cast, the director's job is half done.

Production Organization

During the period when tryouts are taking place, the director can begin to organize other phases of the production. He can distribute copies of the play to faculty members whose classes may have a special interest in the subject matter. He can confer with the school's publicity director, financial manager, and printer, so that they can start the jobs they have in connection with the play.

When floor plans for each set have been agreed upon, the director can begin to make up his prompt book. The prompt book should contain floor plans of the sets, complete blocking of the action, a light plot, a sound plot, a property plot, and all technical cues. The prompt book is the master plan for the production, which the stage manager uses to run the show and from which the plans and cues for all technical phases of the production are taken.

Every text on play direction offers a plan for making a prompt book, and each director will eventually develop his own pattern. The following presents one way to do it.

At the top of an 8½ x 11 inch ditto master, type the following: Title of Play, Act ____, Scene ____, Page ____. Directly under this, make a scale drawing (⅛ inch = 1 foot) of the floor plan of the set, including furniture. Just below the floor plan on the left side of the page, write: Blocking; on the right side write: Technical Cues. Two and one-half inches from the left side of the page, draw a line from the bottom of the floor plan diagram to the bottom of the page. Two inches from the right side of the page, draw a line parallel to the one on the left. Make a similar ditto master for each setting used in the play. On 8½ x 11 inch, unlined, looseleaf notebook paper, ditto as many copies of each setting as there are pages of the script in which that set is used. Cut apart two copies of the printed play and paste each page underneath the appropriate floor plan with rubber cement. (I spent hundreds of hours cutting windows in paper and entangling myself in transparent tape before I realized that it would be wiser to invest in an additional copy of the play!) Assemble and number the pages and put them in a ring binder, with dividers between acts and scenes. In the prompt book, the director's blocking can be written on the left side of the page beside the appropriate line of dialogue and the technical cues on the right side of the page. So that technical cues can be easily identified, light cues may be entered in red, sound and music in blue, and curtain cues in green. The blocking should be done in soft pencil so that it may be changed as rehearsals progress.

Blocking the Play

Blocking, or planning all the movement of actors on the stage, is the responsibility of the director, and should be planned and written in the prompt book before the first rehearsal with the actors. Although a few directors say they want to allow actors the freedom to feel their way into stage positions and relationships, most experienced directors prefer to preblock their shows. Certainly, preblocking saves much rehearsal time for everyone, because the trial and error method is inefficient. Further, how the actor feels about his position on the stage is much less important than how the audience feels about it. The director is a kind of super-audience.

The primary purpose of blocking is to focus the attention of the audience upon whatever character and action is most important at each moment of the play. The director must plan the blocking so the audience will see what he wants them to see and hear what he wants them to hear in order to understand the play. A secondary purpose of blocking is to make the stage pictures attractive or dramatic.

In order to achieve these goals, the director must know and follow the basic rules of stage position, actors' posture, composition, and focus, which are explained in any good directing text. Following are some of the most important of these rules.

> Let the audience see the whole actor. Keep the actors close to the audience and in front of the furniture.
>
> Movement attracts attention. Actors must move on their own lines and remain stationary while others speak.
>
> The face is the most expressive part of the body. Actors should show their faces to the audience as much as possible.
>
> Height attracts attention. An actor standing is stronger than one seated. An actor standing on a platform is stronger yet.
>
> The upstage position is stronger than the downstage positions if there is more than one actor on the stage.
>
> Actors should not cover (stand in front of) one another.
>
> Actors should not be arranged in straight lines, semicircles, or any other formal pattern.
>
> Entrances should not be blocked by actors or furniture.
>
> No actor should move on the stage without a reason. As soon as an actor moves, the audience looks for the reason.

Most directors, in high school and elsewhere, would do well to review these rules from time to time and check their blocking to see whether they are violating any of them.

The mechanics of preblocking are relatively simple. Using the traditional abbreviations (u. for upstage, d. for downstage, c. for center stage, l. for stage left, r. for stage right, and x. for cross), he can quickly note his blocking of the action in the prompt book. On the diagram at the top of each page, it is useful to indicate the position of each character who is onstage when the page begins, by placing his initial at the place on the diagram where he is located. When this is compared with the diagrams on the preceding and following pages, one can quickly see which characters have moved, entered, or left the stage. Noting the positions of actors as he blocks each page will save the director considerable time in preblocking. If he is interrupted in the middle of a scene, he can locate each actor easily when he continues blocking, without going back to the beginning and tracing all the movement. This quick reference is also a great convenience in rehearsals when an actor forgets his blocking or the director wishes to rehearse a short section of the play.

Sample sheets from a prompt book of *Macbeth,* on the following pages, will illustrate this method of preparing the director's script, including blocking and diagraming the action, cutting the play, and planning the technical cues. Following these is a light cue sheet for part of *A Young Lady of Property,* which was made by copying the cues from the right margin of the director's prompt script.

Most high school directors work with so-called acting editions of plays, in which the blocking, business, and sometimes the interpretation of the play, in its original production, are printed in italics between the lines of dialogue. These directions usually contribute more confusion than clarification, and many directors prefer to cross them out of their scripts and instruct their casts to do likewise.

Through the blocking of the action, the director does much to indicate his interpretation of the play. By the focus he creates in each scene, he indicates what he considers most important in that scene. By the positions and movements of the individual characters, he reveals his concept of their emotions, characters, and relationships to others. To the degree that movement reveals the meaning of a play, that movement must be planned by the director if it is to have unity and clarity.

Some directors visualize their stage and characters easily as they preblock; others work better with some visual device to help them. A model set on which toy soldiers are the actors can be useful. A simpler aid to the director is a floor plan laid on a table with various colored buttons or spools of thread used to represent the actors. The ability to visualize movement when preblocking seems to improve with practice, and eventually no aids are needed. Experience also seems to make the director's preblocking more accurate, and the longer he directs, the fewer changes in blocking will be necessary during rehearsals.

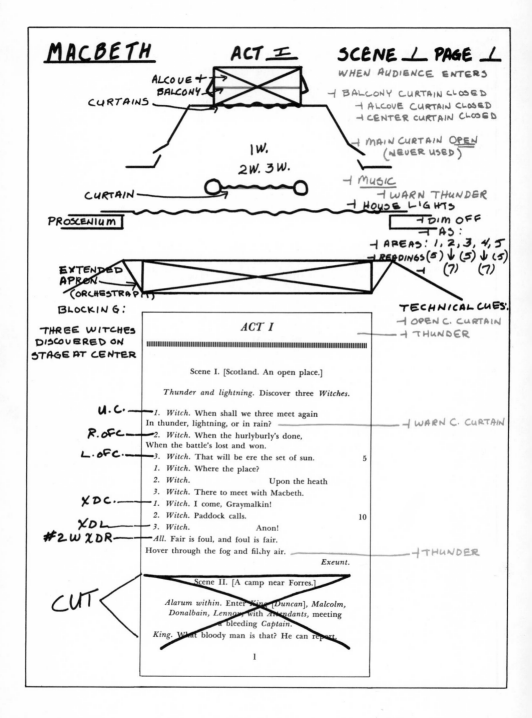

MACBETH — ACT I — SCENE 1 — PAGE 1

WHEN AUDIENCE ENTERS

ALCOVE + BALCONY
CURTAINS

- BALCONY CURTAIN CLOSED
- ALCOVE CURTAIN CLOSED
- CENTER CURTAIN CLOSED
- MAIN CURTAIN OPEN (NEVER USED)

1W. 2W. 3W.

CURTAIN

- MUSIC
- WARN THUNDER
- HOUSE LIGHTS

PROSCENIUM

- DIM OFF
- AS:
- AREAS: 1, 2, 3, 4, 5
- READINGS (5) ↓ (5) ↓ (5)
     (7)   (7)

EXTENDED APRON (ORCHESTRA PIT)

BLOCKING:

THREE WITCHES DISCOVERED ON STAGE AT CENTER

TECHNICAL CUES:
- OPEN C. CURTAIN
- THUNDER

ACT I

Scene I. [Scotland. An open place.]

Thunder and lightning. Discover three *Witches.*

U.C. — *1. Witch.* When shall we three meet again
In thunder, lightning, or in rain? —— — WARN C. CURTAIN
R. OFC. — *2. Witch.* When the hurlyburly's done,
When the battle's lost and won.
L. OFC. — *3. Witch.* That will be ere the set of sun.   5
1. Witch. Where the place?
2. Witch.   Upon the heath
3. Witch. There to meet with Macbeth.
XDC. — *1. Witch.* I come, Graymalkin!
2. Witch. Paddock calls.   10
XDL — *3. Witch.*   Anon!
#2W XDR — *All.* Fair is foul, and foul is fair.
Hover through the fog and filthy air. —— — THUNDER
                         Exeunt.

CUT < Scene II. [A camp near Forres.]

Alarum within. Enter *King* [*Duncan*], Malcolm,
Donalbain, Lennox, with *Attendants,* meeting
a bleeding *Captain.*

King. What bloody man is that? He can report.

1

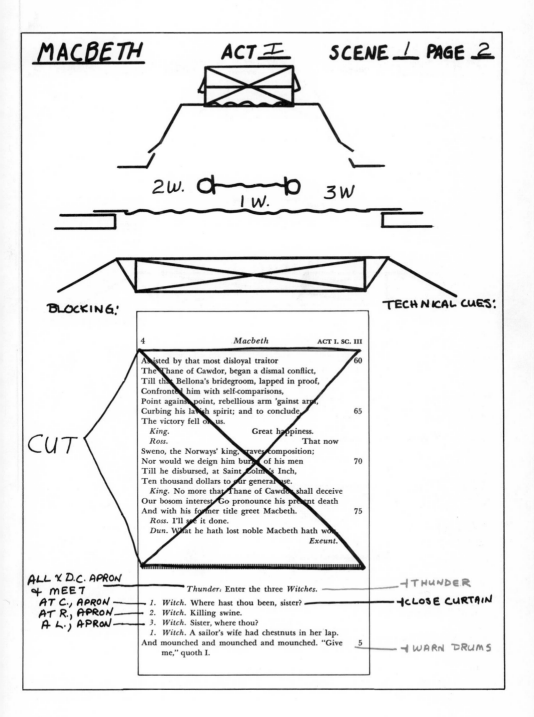

MACBETH   ACT I   SCENE 1 PAGE 2

2W.   1W.   3W

BLOCKING: TECHNICAL CUES:

CUT

4   *Macbeth*   ACT I. SC. III

Assisted by that most disloyal traitor   60
The Thane of Cawdor, began a dismal conflict,
Till that Bellona's bridegroom, lapped in proof,
Confronted him with self-comparisons,
Point against point, rebellious arm 'gainst arm,
Curbing his lavish spirit; and to conclude,   65
The victory fell on us.
    King.   Great happiness.
    Ross.   That now
Sweno, the Norways' king, craves composition;
Nor would we deign him burial of his men   70
Till he disbursed, at Saint Colme's Inch,
Ten thousand dollars to our general use.
    King. No more that Thane of Cawdor shall deceive
Our bosom interest. Go pronounce his present death
And with his former title greet Macbeth.   75
    Ross. I'll see it done.
    Dun. What he hath lost noble Macbeth hath won.
                              Exeunt.

                                                          ┤THUNDER
ALL X D.C. APRON
 ❧ MEET   ── *Thunder.* Enter the three *Witches.* ──
AT C., APRON ──── 1. *Witch.* Where hast thou been, sister? ──── ┤CLOSE CURTAIN
AT R., APRON ──── 2. *Witch.* Killing swine.
A L., APRON ───── 3. *Witch.* Sister, where thou?
                 1. *Witch.* A sailor's wife had chestnuts in her lap.
                 And mounched and mounched and mounched. "Give   5   ── ┤WARN DRUMS
                     me," quoth I.

149

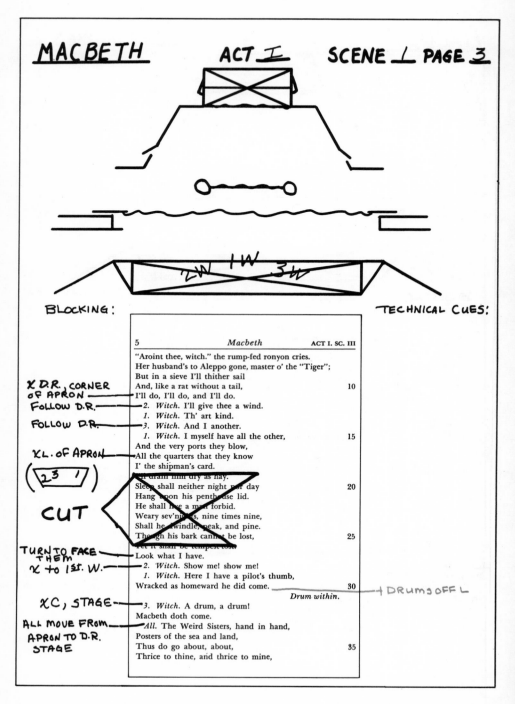

MACBETH ACT I SCENE I PAGE 3

BLOCKING:

TECHNICAL CUES:

X D.R., CORNER
OF APRON ⎯⎯⎯

FOLLOW D.R. ⎯⎯

FOLLOW D.R. ⎯⎯

X L. OF APRON ⎯⎯

(2 3 1)

CUT

TURN TO FACE
THEM ⎯⎯
X to 1ˢᵗ. W. ⎯⎯

XC, STAGE ⎯⎯

ALL MOVE FROM
APRON TO D.R.
STAGE

---

5   *Macbeth*   ACT I. SC. III

"Aroint thee, witch." the rump-fed ronyon cries.
Her husband's to Aleppo gone, master o' the "Tiger";
But in a sieve I'll thither sail
And, like a rat without a tail,   10
I'll do, I'll do, and I'll do.
   2. Witch. I'll give thee a wind.
     1. Witch. Th' art kind.
   3. Witch. And I another.
     1. Witch. I myself have all the other,   15
And the very ports they blow,
All the quarters that they know
I' the shipman's card.
     I'll drain him dry as hay.
Sleep shall neither night nor day   20
Hang upon his penthouse lid.
He shall live a man forbid.
Weary sev'nights, nine times nine,
Shall he dwindle, peak, and pine.
Though his bark cannot be lost,   25
Yet it shall be tempest-tost.
Look what I have.
   2. Witch. Show me! show me!
     1. Witch. Here I have a pilot's thumb,
Wracked as homeward he did come.   30
              Drum within.   + DRUMS OFF L
   3. Witch. A drum, a drum!
Macbeth doth come.
   All. The Weird Sisters, hand in hand,
Posters of the sea and land,
Thus do go about, about,   35
Thrice to thine, and thrice to mine,

MACBETH ACT I SCENE 1 PAGE 4

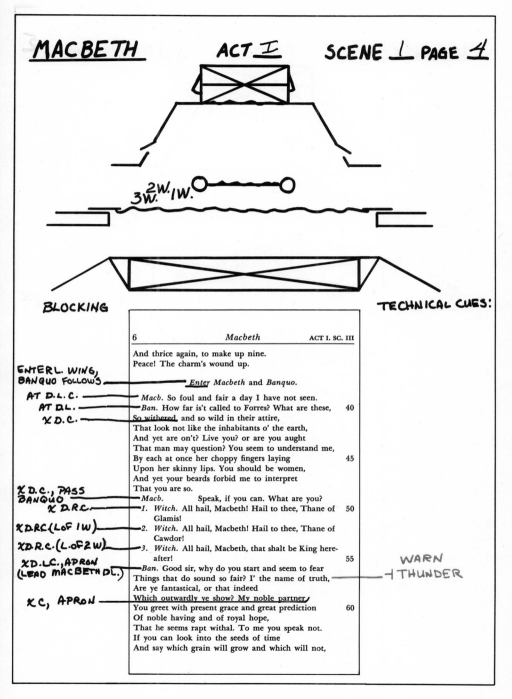

BLOCKING

TECHNICAL CUES:

ENTER L. WING,
BANQUO FOLLOWS

AT D.L.C.

AT D.L.

X D.C.

X D.C., PASS
BANQUO

X D.R.C.

XD.R.C.(L OF 1W)

XD.R.C. (L. OF 2 W)

XD.L.C., APRON
(LEAD MACBETH DL.)

X C, APRON

WARN
+ THUNDER

---

6   *Macbeth*   ACT I. SC. III

And thrice again, to make up nine.
Peace! The charm's wound up.

            Enter Macbeth and Banquo.

Macb. So foul and fair a day I have not seen.
Ban. How far is't called to Forres? What are these,   40
So withered, and so wild in their attire,
That look not like the inhabitants o' the earth,
And yet are on't? Live you? or are you aught
That man may question? You seem to understand me,
By each at once her choppy fingers laying   45
Upon her skinny lips. You should be women,
And yet your beards forbid me to interpret
That you are so.
Macb.   Speak, if you can. What are you?
1. Witch. All hail, Macbeth! Hail to thee, Thane of   50
    Glamis!
2. Witch. All hail, Macbeth! Hail to thee, Thane of
    Cawdor!
3. Witch. All hail, Macbeth, that shalt be King here-
    after!   55
Ban. Good sir, why do you start and seem to fear
Things that do sound so fair? I' the name of truth,
Are ye fantastical, or that indeed
Which outwardly ye show? My noble partner
You greet with present grace and great prediction   60
Of noble having and of royal hope,
That he seems rapt withal. To me you speak not.
If you can look into the seeds of time
And say which grain will grow and which will not,

MACBETH ACT I SCENE 1 PAGE 5

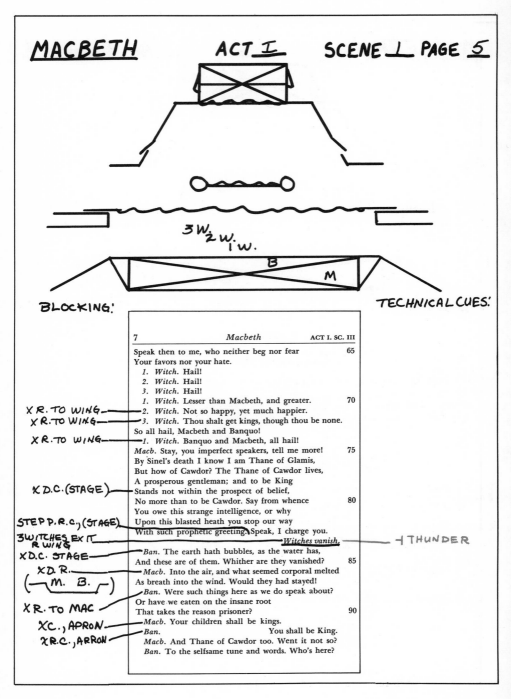

3 W.
2 W.
1 W.

B M

BLOCKING:

X R. TO WING
X R. TO WING
X R. TO WING

X D.C. (STAGE)

STEP P.R.C., (STAGE)
3 WITCHES EXIT
R WING
X D.C. STAGE
X D. R.
(M. B.)

X R. TO MAC
X C., APRON
X R.C., APRON

TECHNICAL CUES:

THUNDER

---

7   *Macbeth*   ACT I. SC. III

Speak then to me, who neither beg nor fear   65
Your favors nor your hate.
  1. Witch. Hail!
  2. Witch. Hail!
  3. Witch. Hail!
  1. Witch. Lesser than Macbeth, and greater.   70
  2. Witch. Not so happy, yet much happier.
  3. Witch. Thou shalt get kings, though thou be none.
So all hail, Macbeth and Banquo!
  1. Witch. Banquo and Macbeth, all hail!
Macb. Stay, you imperfect speakers, tell me more!   75
By Sinel's death I know I am Thane of Glamis,
But how of Cawdor? The Thane of Cawdor lives,
A prosperous gentleman; and to be King
Stands not within the prospect of belief,
No more than to be Cawdor. Say from whence   80
You owe this strange intelligence, or why
Upon this blasted heath you stop our way
With such prophetic greeting. Speak, I charge you.
            Witches vanish.
Ban. The earth hath bubbles, as the water has,
And these are of them. Whither are they vanished?   85
Macb. Into the air, and what seemed corporal melted
As breath into the wind. Would they had stayed!
Ban. Were such things here as we do speak about?
Or have we eaten on the insane root
That takes the reason prisoner?   90
Macb. Your children shall be kings.
Ban.   You shall be King.
Macb. And Thane of Cawdor too. Went it not so?
Ban. To the selfsame tune and words. Who's here?

Young Lady of Property			*Light Cues*
Cue Number	*Page Number*	*Cue*	*Light Changes*
1	3	Overture music begins	Dim house ½
2	3	1½ minute overture	Begin dim house out
3	3	1½ minute overture	Fade in areas 2, 4
4	3	2 minute overture	House out and warn area 4
5	3	*Russell*—The Bobbsey Twins	Dim area 4 out
6	4	*Wilma*—Come on, Arabella	Warn area 4
7	5	*Wilma*—Letter in General Delivery	Warn area 2
8	5	*Martha*—Found any mail	Dim in area 4
9	5	*Wilma*—I'd like to scratch	Dim area 2 out
10	8	*Lester*—Hanging around the streets	Warn areas 4, 1
11	9	Lester and Mrs. Leighton exit DR	Crossfade—4 out, 1 in
12	12	*Minna*—Stop talking crazy	Warn area 1
13	13	*Minna*—Get right back	Fade area 1 to blackout
14	13	Count 5 in blackout	Fade area 1 in
15	15	*Gert*—Oh hello, Miss Martha	Warn areas 1, 3
16	16	*Gert*—What can you do?	Crossfade—1 out, 3 in
17	20	*Wilma*—You're not telling me	Warn areas 3, 1
18	21	*Arabella*—Don't say I said it	Crossfade—3 out, 1 in
19	25	*Minna*—You know your daddy	Warn area 1
20	26	*Minna*—You come back here	Fade area 1 to blackout

Rehearsing the Play

Once the casting and preblocking have been completed, it takes approximately one hundred hours of rehearsal to prepare a full-length play for production, whether the rehearsal hours are spread over twelve weeks or two. Because the student actors have classes to keep up with, the two-week rehearsal period is impractical, of course. Five or six weeks seems to be the ideal rehearsal time for a high school play, with rehearsals held for two or three hours, five days each week except the last. Weekend rehearsals should be held just before the production, so that student actors and crews don't lose their momentum or concentration. Although the rehearsal period may be extended to seven or eight weeks for a very difficult show, a longer rehearsal period usually does not produce better results. Students, and perhaps directors as well, seem to work better under pressure, and they do not begin to work seriously until they realize they have barely enough time to get the job done.

Periodically during the rehearsal period, the director must confer with the other faculty members involved and with the student crews to be sure that all phases of the production are progressing according to schedule. Among other things, he must check on the colors to be used in the set and costumes to be sure that they contribute to the mood and interpretation toward which he and the actors are working. He must also check on the publicity, set construction, printing, and lighting. If the production is well organized and a good staff has been obtained, this checking will not consume much of the director's time. The constant checking is necessary, however, because the director will have to see that each job is completed, even if the person responsible for it fails. He cannot do the show in the dark because the light crew failed at its job. When I arrived for the first technical rehearsal of *Medea,* the crew proudly showed me the two most magnificent snakes any stage has ever seen twined around the pillars at the entrance to Medea's house. At the touch of a button, they wiggled, their eyes shone red, and smoke poured from their fangs! But not a single light had been hung, set, or gelled. An earlier check on the light crew would have been wise.

The company reading, which is held at the first rehearsal of many plays, is an unnecessary waste of time for the high school play. The actors have already read the entire play, and the director has discussed his interpretation of the play during tryouts. High school students tend to be restless and inattentive if a company reading is held and subtle interpretations of the characters are discussed. They don't realize that they will have any problems until they actually confront them, much later in the rehearsal period.

At the first rehearsal of the play, the blocking of the action begins. If the director has done his homework, this can be a speedy process.

All actors in the first act, or scene, should be seated with play scripts and pencils in hand to record the blocking as it is dictated by the director. When actors have written their blocking for the first act, they should go onstage and walk through the action as they read their lines. During this first walk-through of blocking, the director should watch the actors and the script very carefully to be sure that it is correctly understood and executed. At the same rehearsal, actors should walk through the blocked act a second time, in order to set it in their minds and relate it to the dialogue. This same procedure should be followed at the next rehearsals with the subsequent scenes, until the entire play has been blocked. Ordinarily, a week is enough time for blocking a full-length play.

The next step in the rehearsal process is memorization of lines. Student actors should be told not to begin memorizing their lines until after they have been through the blocking of each act. There are two reasons for this. First, they will learn both lines and blocking more thoroughly if they learn them together. Second, the blocking will often reveal the proper interpretation of a line or scene and therefore make it easier to memorize. A week and a half to two weeks should be spent concentrating on memorizing the play. Perhaps two days' rehearsal of each act individually, running through it two or three times, and three rehearsals running through the entire play will suffice. During the memorization rehearsals, the director should not interrupt the actors, unless there are gross errors in blocking or interpretation. Frequent stops slow down the learning process. During these rehearsals, actors should not carry their scripts on stage but should ask the stage manager for a line when they cannot think of it. Gradually the prompting will become less frequent. No prompting should be permitted during the last week of rehearsals or during performances. If actors are allowed a prompter, they will depend upon him. If they have no prompter, they will learn to ad lib their way out of any difficulty that arises.

Many directors over-direct their actors by expecting too much of them too early in the rehearsals. They try to do everything—blocking, characterization, interpretation, and pacing—at the same time. The result is that they confuse the actors and accomplish almost nothing. If the director can refrain from helping the actors during the weeks when they are blocking and memorizing the show, he will discover that they will grow and develop in their characterizations while they rehearse. By the third week of rehearsal, the actors will have discovered for themselves most of the things a director wants to tell them at the third rehearsal. During this first half of the rehearsal period, the director should, of course, answer any questions his actors have, but he should not look for things to direct.

When the director feels that the actors have exhausted their own resources in developing their characterizations, he should begin to help them. His help will be most effective if it expands the actor's understanding of the motivations of his character rather than offering external directions to move faster or look happier. The director can help an actor by asking him questions about how his character feels and why he behaves as he does, and by discussing other ways the character might feel or behave. Most actors do communicate their understanding of the character they are playing to the audience. If the director can help the actor understand his role in the same way the director understands it, the actor will usually be able to play the role to the director's satisfaction. The director should never read a line for an actor, and should rarely demonstrate an action or gesture. If the actor cannot understand the meaning of a line, he will not be able to read it correctly by rote. His imitation of the director's reading will be hollow and unconvincing. Likewise, the gesture that does not grow out of the actor's understanding of his character will look artificial. The more perceptive members of the audience will be able to tell that the line reading or the gesture has been "hung on" the actor by the director!

How the director divides the rehearsal time during the last half of the rehearsal period will depend partly upon the needs of the particular play being presented. Some plays will require special attention to dialects, others to voice development, others to phrasing. All will require that some rehearsals be spent sharpening characterizations, pacing the show, and integrating the technical aspects of the production. Whatever the needs of the show, maximum progress and improvement will be made, if the director works on one aspect at a time. At some rehearsals he may concentrate on speech and dialect, at others on characterization, and at others on tempo.

In every case, the director must have completed all his work with the actors before the final week of rehearsals. During that week, both director and actors must concentrate on the technical aspects of production —properties, setting, costumes, makeup, music, sound effects, and lighting. All these things must be painstakingly rehearsed if the production is to be effective. The director should, of course, give the actors notes on those things he observes during the final rehearsals, and at the last dress rehearsal, he should take extensive notes on every aspect of the production.

The greatest aid to improving the quality of the shows, in my opinion, is an office-type or a cassette tape recorder. Once the show has been blocked and memorized, it can be used at nearly every rehearsal. An office tape recorder or cassette is suggested, because it can be started and stopped by a button on the hand microphone. With this microphone in hand, a director can watch the rehearsals and record his reactions and suggestions, taking many more and much better notes at a single rehearsal than with a pencil and clipboard. More importantly, when the tape is played back to the students at the end of each rehearsal, they are able to understand his emotional reactions to the play, as well as his ideas and suggestions for improvement. No recap of written notes can communicate as clearly to the cast as the director's emotion-charged voice on a tape recorder! I recommend it to every director who wants to produce more highly polished shows, whether they be in a high school or in a professional theatre.

The director should not consider his job finished when the curtain rises on the first performance of his play. Rather, he should sit with the audience at every performance to discover whether they respond as he and his company wanted them to respond. If they do not, the director must analyze the response and the production in order to make changes and adjustments that will evoke the desired response from the next audience. The conscientious director and his students will use each performance as a laboratory in which to test and improve their interpretations of the play. Even after the final performance, the director should attempt to assess the strengths and weaknesses of his production for his own benefit and that of his students.

For the audience, the actors, and the director, the production of plays in a high school can be meaningful and memorable. Theatre experience, either as participant or auditor, can provide insights into life, self, and society, which help to develop more intelligent and compassionate human beings.

For the high school director, offering theatrical experiences that reveal some of the meaning of life and teach students compassionate understanding of others is a work worth all the energy it requires. It matters permanently!

Suggested Reading for
Drama Students

The following plays are suggested for reading by drama students because of their recognized quality as representative pieces of dramatic literature. Plays *not* on this list will *not* be accepted for play reports, unless the student presents advance notice to the teacher and receives written approval from *both* his teacher and his parent or guardian.

Greek Period

Aeschylus
  Prometheus Bound
  Agamemnon

Sophocles
  Oedipus the King
  Antigone (Jean Anouilh)

Euripides
  Medea (Robinson Jeffers)
  Alcestis
  Electra
  The Trojan Women

Aristophanes
  The Clouds
  The Birds
  The Frogs

Medieval Period

  Everyman (Anonymous)

Elizabethan Period

Shakespeare
  Much Ado About Nothing
  Romeo and Juliet
  King Richard II and *III*
  Hamlet
  Othello
  King Lear
  Macbeth
  Anthony and Cleopatra
  The Comedy of Errors
  The Taming of the Shrew
  A Midsummer Night's Dream
  The Merchant of Venice

As You Like It
Twelfth Night
The Tempest

Ben Jonson
Volpone
The Alchemist

Christopher Marlowe
Dr. Faustus

French Period—Seventeenth Century

Molière
The Imaginary Invalid
Tartuffe
The Doctor in Spite of Himself
The Miser
The Bourgeois Gentleman
The Misanthrope
The School for Wives

Restoration Period

William Congreve
The Way of the World

Eighteenth Century

Oliver Goldsmith
She Stoops to Conquer

Richard Brinsley Sheridan
The School for Scandal
The Rivals

Modern Period
BEFORE 1920 (approximately)

Henrik Ibsen (Norwegian)
An Enemy of the People
The Pillars of Society
Hedda Gabler
The Wild Duck
A Doll's House
Ghosts
The Master Builder
Peer Gynt

Anton Chekhov (Russian)
The Cherry Orchard
The Sea Gull
Uncle Vanya
The Three Sisters

Edmond Rostand (French)
Cyrano de Bergerac
The Romancers

Ferenc Molnar (Hungarian)
Liliom
The Guardsman

Karel Čapek (Czechoslovakian)
R.U.R
The Insect Comedy

George Bernard Shaw (Irish)
Saint Joan
Candida
Arms and the Man
Caesar and Cleopatra
Pygmalion
Androcles and the Lion
The Devil's Disciple
Man and Superman
Major Barbara

Nikolai Gogol (Russian)
The Inspector General

Oscar Wilde (Irish by birth)
The Importance of Being Earnest
Lady Windermere's Fan

J. M. Barrie (Scotch)
Dear Brutus
Quality Street
The Admirable Crichton
Peter Pan
What Every Woman Knows

John Galsworthy (English)
Escape
Strife
The Silver Box
Justice

Sean O'Casey (Irish)
Juno and the Paycock
The Plough and the Stars

Federico Garcia Lorca (Spanish)
Blood Wedding
The House of Bernarda Alba
AFTER 1920 (approximately)

Eugene O'Neill (American)
Ah, Wilderness!

NOTE TO STUDENTS AND PARENTS:

Beyond the Horizon
The Iceman Cometh
Long Day's Journey Into
*   Night*
Anna Christie
Strange Interlude
Mourning Becomes Electra
Desire Under the Elms
All God's Chillun Got Wings

Thornton Wilder (American)
The Skin of Our Teeth
The Matchmaker
Our Town

Arthur Miller (American)
Death of a Salesman
The Crucible
All My Sons

Noel Coward (English)
Blythe Spirit
Cavalcade
Private Lives

Elmer Rice (American)
The Adding Machine
Street Scene

Maxwell Anderson (American)
What Price Glory
Elizabeth The Queen
Joan of Lorraine
Barefoot in Athens
Mary of Scotland
Winterset
High Tor
The Bad Seed
Star Wagon

Robert B. Sherwood (American)
Abe Lincoln in Illinois
Petrified Forest
Idiot's Delight
There Shall Be No Night

William Saroyan (American)
My Heart's in the Highlands
The Time of Your Life

Paul Osborne (American)
On Borrowed Time
Point of No Return
Bell for Adano

T. S. Eliot (English–born
    American)
Murder in the Cathedral
The Family Reunion

Christopher Fry (English)
The Lady's Not for Burning
The First Born

Kaufman and Hart (American)
George Washington Slept
*   Here*
The Man Who Came to
*   Dinner*
You Can't Take It With You
I'd Rather Be Right
The American Way

Marc Connelly (American)
Green Pastures
Beggar on Horseback
(with Kaufman)

Kaufman and Ferber (American)
Stage Door
The Royal Family
Dinner at Eight

Tennessee Williams (American)
The Glass Menagerie
Summer and Smoke

Carson McCullers (American)
The Member of the Wedding

Phillip Barry (American)
Holiday
The Philadelphia Story
The Youngest
Paris Bound
The Animal Kingdom
Here Come the Clowns

John Van Druten (American)
I Remember Mama
Bell, Book and Candle

Clifford Odets (American)
Golden Boy
The Country Girl

Lillian Hellman (American)
The Little Foxes
Watch on the Rhine

John Patrick (American)
The Hasty Heart
Teahouse of the August Moon
The Curious Savage

Paul Green (American)
In Abraham's Bosom
The Field God
Lonesome Road

Paul Vincent Carrol (Irish)
Shadow and Substance
The White Steed

Coffee and Cowen (American)
Family Portrait

G. Martinez Sierra (Spanish)
The Kingdom of God
The Cradle Song

Jean Anouilh (French)
Thieves Carnival
Ring Round the Moon
Time Remembered
The Lark

Ryerson and Clements (American)
Harriet

Lawrence and Lee (American)
Inherit the Wind

Emlyn Williams (English)
Night Must Fall

Dore Schary (American)
The Highest Tree
Sunrise at Campobello

Sidney Howard (American)
The Late Christopher Bean
The Yellow Jacket

Terence Rattigan (English)
The Winslow Boy

Sutton Vane (English)
Outward Bound

Patterson Greene (American)
Papa is All

John Balderston (English)
Berkeley Square

Coxe and Chapman (American)
Billy Budd

Goodrich and Hackett (American)
The Diary of Anne Frank
The Great Big Doorstep

Brian Doherty (American)
Father Malachy's Miracle

Channing Pollock (American)
The Fool

Fay Kanin (American)
Good-bye My Fancy

Truman Capote (American)
The Grass Harp

Leonid Andreyev (Russian)
He Who Gets Slapped

Ruth and August Goetz (American)
The Heiress

Edward Chodorov (American)
Kind Lady

Rotter and Vincent (Polish & German)
Letters to Lucerne

S. E. Hsung (American)
Lady Precious Stream

Lindsay and Crouse (American)
Life With Father

Emmet Lavery (American)
The Magnificent Yankee

Thurber and Nugent (American)
The Male Animal

Robinson Jeffers (American)
Medea

A. A. Milne (English)
Mr. Pim Passes By

Mary Chase (American)
Bernardine
Mrs. McThing
Harvey

André Obey (French)
Noah

E. P. Conkle (American)
Prologue to Glory

Edith Sommer (American)
Room Full of Roses

Charles Rann Kennedy
(English)
Servant in the House

Ruth Gordon (American)
Years Ago

Guy Bolton (American)
Anastasia

Rudolph Besier (English)
Barretts of Wimpole Street

William Gibson (American)
Miracle Worker

Lorraine Hansberry (American)
Raisin in the Sun

Ketti Frings (American)
Look Homeward Angel

Herman Wouk (American)
*The Caine Mutiny Court-
Martial*

Jean Giraudoux (French)
The Madwoman of Chaillot
Tiger at the Gates

Publicity Summary
The Grass Harp

To: Newspapers, Administration, Journalism Department, Public Relations Director

FROM: Charlotte Kay Motter, Director

The information contained herein is designed to give all concerned with the promotion and publicity of plays presented by Canoga Park High School the background data concerning this production.

TITLE OF PLAY: *The Grass Harp*

PLAYWRIGHT: Truman Capote

PERFORMANCE DATES: Student Matinees: May 2 and 3, 1968— extended period 6

Evening: Saturday, May 4, 1968—8:15 P.M.

ADMISSION: Students: 50¢
Adults: $1.00

CONTENTS: The Cast
The Playwright
The Play
The Characters
The Actors
The Director and Staff

The Cast

(in order of appearance)

Catherine Creek	Rachel Levario
Collin Talbo	John Cristofil
Dolly Talbo	Carolyn Daugherty
Verina Talbo	Adrienne Herdzina
Dr. Morris Ritz	Jerry Anderson
The Reverend's Wife	Carol Petti
The Reverend	Ron Kenzer
The Barber	Ron Zarro
The Baker's Wife	Peggy Mills
The Postmistress	Sherry DeBruhl
The Sheriff	Garry Collins
Judge Charlie Cool	Steve Habbershaw
The Choir Mistress	June Hart
Big Eddie Stover	Darryl Cordle
Brophy	Jim James
Sam	Pat McLynn
Maude Riordan	Ellen Epstein
Miss Baby Love Dallas	Patt Henderson

The Playwright

Born in 1923, Truman Capote has been an important American writer of short stories, novels, plays, and television dramas for more than twenty years. He has received the O. Henry Award and the Creative Writing Award of the National Institution of Arts and Letters. In 1948 his first novel, *Other Voices, Other Rooms,* brought him wide recognition. *The Grass Harp,* adapted from his own novel of the same title, was his first play. He has since written *The Muses Are Heard, Breakfast at Tiffany's,* and the best selling *In Cold Blood.* Two television dramas presented last December showed him to be one of the masters of that medium: *Among the Paths to Eden,* and *A Christmas Memory,* a rebroadcast of his 1966 Emmy Award winner.

The Play

The Grass Harp is a simple, whimsical story of two spinster sisters in a small southern town. One is an aggressive realist, the other a withdrawn idealist. In a sense they symbolize "the Establishment" in conflict with "the Hippie Generation." As portrayed by Capote in this highly autobiographical work, each emerges as a valuable human being who cannot exist without the other.

The Grass Harp was originally produced by Saint-Subber in Association with Rita Allen at the Martin Beck Theatre in New York in 1952. It was directed by Robert Lewis. It was Capote's first play and considered by the playwright and by most critics to be a failure. Audiences, however, were touched and amused by the play. Brooks Atkinson, dean of drama critics, agreed that *The Grass Harp* was well worth producing.

Saint-Subber has said that to produce *The Grass Harp* was the "fulfillment of an aesthetic desire, of a need to introduce a new theatre talent, Truman Capote." It is a universal play about universal people. It has something to say to everybody.

The Grass Harp has been chosen for production at this high school at this time because it is a play about beauty of spirit and love of life. It is "where the younger generation is at." Some of them may be surprised to learn that the playwright, an "old" man of forty-four, is there also.

The Characters

DOLLY TALBO.   A quiet, delicate, eccentric lady who cannot bear any harshness in her world. She makes a home-cooked herb cure for dropsy, from a secret formula given her by gypsies, which she sells by mail orders. As described by Capote, ". . . her presence is a delicate happening. . . . Her movements are quick and yet uncertain. It disturbs her to make the most ordinary decision—whether to place a saucer here, a fork there."

VERINA TALBO.   A strong, business-like woman. ". . . she walks as though she were part of a slow and haughty procession; her posture is severe, her manner exalted." The opposite of her sister Dolly in every detail.

COLLIN TALBO.   The fifteen year old nephew of the two sisters, who has been reared by them. He is a dreamer like Dolly, and a school drop-out. He tries to be a "hard guy" but is actually very sensitive and loyal to his family.

CATHERINE CREEK.   Servant to the Talbo family and close companion of Dolly and Collin. Catherine is a witty, kind, large Negro woman who pretends to be an Indian.

DR. MORRIS RITZ.   A con man who poses as a chemical engineer, and plans with Verina to get Dolly's dropsy formula and mass-produce it. Failing to do this, he steals all of Verina's money and leaves town.

JUDGE CHARLIE COOL.   A retired judge who is seeking peace and "the one person in the world to whom he can tell everything" so he won't be lonely any more.

THE TOWNSPEOPLE.   A group of people consisting of every type known to man. They include a reverend and his wife, a barber, a baker's wife, a postmistress, a sheriff and his posse, a choir mistress, a door-to-door saleswoman, and Collin's girlfriend.

The Actors

CAROLYN DAUGHERTY.   Carolyn, who plays Dolly Talbo, has previously appeared in "The Sandbox," *Our Town,* done as a concert reading, and *The Child Buyer*. She also holds several speech awards.

ADRIENNE HERDZINA. Adrienne has taken major roles in the one-act play, "The Boor," *Our Town,* done as a concert reading, *The Child Buyer,* and *Major Barbara,* done as a concert reading also. In this play, she will take on the role of Verina Talbo.

RACHEL LEVARIO. As Rachel's first leading role, she will play the part of Catherine Creek. She has also served as stage manager for *The Miracle Worker* and student director for *Major Barbara.*

JOHN CHRISTOFIL. John is at the present taking the part of Collin Talbo. In the past, he played in *The Child Buyer* and has also worked as a stage hand.

STEVE HABBERSHAW. Steve has previously been seen as the butler in *The Importance of Being Earnest* for which he was also assistant stage manager, the child buyer in *The Child Buyer,* and an owner of a factory manufacturing articles of war in *Major Barbara.* He now holds the part of a retired judge, Judge Charlie Cool.

The Staff

DIRECTOR:

Miss Charlotte Kay Motter has been drama teacher at Canoga Park High School for the past eighteen years. She recently presided as the newly elected president at the first statewide meeting of the California Educational Theatre Association held in San Diego, March 29 through 31. She delivered a position paper on theatre education that she presented to the state board of education. In 1961, Miss Motter received the Freedom Foundation's Classroom Teacher's Medal for her program of plays concerning democratic ideals. She is listed in *Who's Who in American Theatre* and was President of the Drama Teacher's Association of Southern California and the Southern California District of AETA. Miss Motter is currently writing a textbook to be published by Prentice-Hall in 1970. It encompasses her experiences and philosophy of theatre education, and as the first volume of its kind, is directed toward assisting secondary school drama teachers in their efforts to provide children with an educationally valuable program in drama.

CREWS:

Miss Jacqueline Melvin, publicity director for Canoga Park High School, is supervisor for the drama department's prop, costume, makeup, and publicity crews. She is also director of the one-act invitational plays produced by the Drama II classes.

SETS:

Mr. Al Carrillo, art department chairman, supervises the designing of all the sets used in the one-act plays and the full-length school productions. Mr. Carillo's stage design classes work in conjunction with Miss Motter's stagecraft classes to do the basic construction of the sets.

Canoga Park High School Special Bulletin

DATE: April 19, 1965
TO: Faculty, Parents, and Students
FROM: Charlotte Kay Motter, Director
APPROVED: A. C. Dartt, Girls' Vice Principal

SUBJECT: Rehearsal & Production Schedule for *Look Homeward Angel*

Date	Time	Scenes	Cast	Crew	Purpose	Notes
Mon. 4/19	3:15-5:00	I, 1	I, 1	Stg. mgrs.	Blocking	Order tickets
Tues. 4/20	3:15-5:00	I, 1	I, 1	Stg. mgrs.	Blocking	Complete set design
Wed. 4/21	3:15-5:00	I, 1	I, 1	Stg. mgrs.	Run twice	Begin program copy
Thurs. 4/22	3:15-5:00	I, 2	I, 2	Stg. mgrs.	Blocking	Begin cost. & props
Friday 4/23	3:15-5:00	I, 2	I, 2	Stg. mgrs.	Run twice	Stage crew *daily* until finish
Mon. 4/26	3:15-5:30	I, 1 & 2	I, 1 & 2	Stg. mgrs.	Memorized	Begin set constr.
Tues. 4/27	3:15-5:30	II, 1 & 2	II, 1 & 2	Stg. mgrs.	Blocking	Begin light plot
Wed. 4/28	3:15-5:30	II, 1 & 2	II, 1 & 2	Stg. mgrs.	Blocking	Order mailers
Thurs. 4/29	3:15-5:30	III	III	Stg. mgrs.	Blocking	
Friday 4/30	3:15-5:00	III	III	Stg. mgrs.	Blocking	
Mon. 5/3	3:15-6:00	II, 1 & 2	II, 1 & 2	Stg. mgrs.	Memorized	Begin painting
Tues. 5/4	3:15-5:30	III	III	Stg. mgrs.	Memorized	Request hall signs, etc.
Wed. 5/5	3:15-6:00	I, 1 & 2	I, 1 & 2	Stg. mgrs.	Run thru	Organize ticket sales
Thurs. 5/6	3:15-6:00	II, 1 & 2	II, 1 & 2	Stg. mgrs.	Run thru	Haul in set
Friday 5/7	3:15-4:10	III	III	Stg. mgrs.	Run thru	Order costumes, makeup

Date	Time	Scenes	Cast	Crew	Purpose	Notes
Mon. 5/10	NO REHEARSAL—NOON PLAY DRESS & TECH.				PICK UP MAILERS	
Tues. 5/11	3:15-6:00	All	All	Stg. mgrs.	Run thru	Address mailers
Wed. 5/12	3:15-6:00	All	All	Stg. mgrs.	Run thru	Order programs
Thurs. 5/13	3:15-6:00	All	All	Stg. mgrs.	Run thru	Pick up tickets
Friday 5/14	3:15-6:00	All	All	All	Run thru	Crews see show & check plans
Sat. 5/15	2:00-6:00	All	All	Stg. mgrs.	Character	
Mon. 5/17	3:15-6:00	All	All	Stg. mgrs.	Pace	Begin ticket sales
Tues. 5/18	3:15-6:00	All	All	Stg. & prop.	Props	Finish painting
Wed. 5/19	3:15-6:00	All	All	Stg. & prop.	Light & sound	Mail mailers
Thurs. 5/20	3:15- ?	All	All	Stg. & prop.	Full tech.	*Bring food!*
Friday 5/21	SENIOR PROM—NO REHEARSAL—*PICK UP COSTUMES*					
Sat. 5/22	7:00-12:00	All	All	All	Costumes	
Sun. 5/23	1:30-6:00	All	All	All	Make up	
Mon. 5/24	5:00-10:00	All	All	All	Dress	
Tues. 5/25	5:00-9:00	All	All	All	Dress	Pick up programs
Wed. 5/26	10:15-3:30	All	All	All	Matinee	
Thurs. 5/27	10:15-5:30	All	All	All	Matinee	Pictures—cast & crew
Friday 5/28	10:15-3:30	All	All	All	Matinee	
Sat. 5/29	6:30-12:00	All	All	All	Evening	Strike set, props

CAST AND CREW PARTY UNTIL 2:00 A.M. ONLY! NO GUESTS!

| Mon. 5/31 | NO SCHOOL | | | | | |
| Tues. 6/1 | Complete return of props, costumes, and clean shop. | | | | | |

Los Angeles City School Districts

Canoga Park High School

6850 Topanga Canyon Boulevard, Canoga Park, California

JACK P. CROWTHER
Superintendent of Schools

BROOKS E. WILLIAMS
Principal

My dear _____:

As a major portion of the semester assignment in Play Production, _____ has been cast in the role of _____ in the play_____, which will be presented_____. The time spent in rehearsals for this production will, for the most part, replace the time required for home study in other classes which grant a like amount of school credit to their students. As you may know, the suggested optimum number of hours of homework in the English classes in the Los Angeles City High Schools is one hour for each class period, or approximately one hundred hours each semester. Play Production is an English elective course.

It is my hope that the members of this group will be able to maintain the high quality of production achieved by past Play Production students here.

The school's purpose in including the production of plays in its regular course of instruction is neither to raise funds nor to train students for the entertainment profession, but rather to enrich the cultural experiences of all of the students at Canoga, both participants and audience as part of their general education in the humanities.

Your understanding of and co-operation in enforcing the following rules of conduct will be of immeasurable assistance and will be genuinely appreciated: 1. Promptness at all rehearsals; 2. Attendance at all rehearsals required; 3. Notification of director when tardiness or absence is unavoidable. (School Phone: DI 0-3221) 4. Absolutely no drinking before or during rehearsals, performances, or the cast party; 5. No smoking in the auditorium or on the school grounds at any time. Violation of these rules will result in the student being dropped from the class without credit.

You may be assured that I never leave a rehearsal until I am sure that every student is on his way home.

I have attached hereto a complete rehearsal schedule with the times when_____ will be needed encircled in red pencil. After you have read it, will you be so kind as to fill in the enclosed blank, sign it, and return it to me as soon as possible.

Respectfully yours,

Charlotte Kay Motter
Drama Director

Short Plays Recommended for High School

Title	Playwright	Cast		Type	Comment
A Pound on Demand	O'Casey	3M	1F	Comedy	Two excellent male roles; Irish dialect
Trifles	Glaspell	3M	2F	Melodrama	Two excellent female roles; suspense
Sorry, Wrong Number	Fletcher	3M	1F	Melodrama	Chiller; almost all female monologue
The Stronger	Strindberg		2F	Drama	Excellent exercise; for two actresses
Here We Are	Parker	1M	1F	Comedy	Honeymoon fight
A Sunny Morning	Quintero	2M	2F	Comedy	Leading roles are elderly, delicate
The Long Stay Cut Short	Williams	1M	2F	Drama	Folk characters, poverty area
Mooney's Kid Don't Cry	Williams	1M	1F	Drama	Conflict between dreams and reality in life
The Trysting Place	Tarkington	4M	3F	Comedy	Courtship is funny, at any age
Aria da Capo	Millay	4M	1F	Drama	Commedia dell' arte style
The Village Wooing	Shaw	1M	1F extras	Comedy	Sentimental, but still Shaw
Everyman	Unknown	4M	12F	Drama	Morality play
A Young Lady of Property	Foote	3M	6F	Drama	Loneliness of a Texas orphan
Thursday Evening	Morley	1M	3F	Comedy	A mother-in-law story
Martha and Mary	Box		7F	Religious	At the grave of Jesus

Title	Playwright	Cast		Type	Comment
Poor Aubrey	Kelly	1M	3F	Comedy	Character on which *The Show Off* is based
The Undercurrent	Ehlert	2M	4F	Drama	Problem of juvenile delinquency; German accent
The Boor	Chekhov	1M	1F extras	Farce	Two difficult, comic roles
Overtones	Gerstenberg		4F	Comedy	Ladies at tea bring other selves
The Twelve Pound Look	Barrie	2M	2F	Comedy	How can a "lady" earn her own living?
Suppressed Desires	Glaspell	1M	2F	Comedy	Satire on psychoanalysis
The Case of the Crushed Petunias	Williams	2M	2F	Comedy	Whimsical conflict between a puritan and a libertine
Dark Lady of the Sonnets	Shaw	2M	2F	Comedy	Satire on Shakespeare's creative genius and his love life
The Dancers	Foote	3M	7F	Comedy	Realistic story of shy teenagers
The Flattering Word	Kelly	2M	3F	Comedy	Observation of human foibles
Riders to the Sea	Synge	1M	3F extras	Tragedy	Folk tale of fishermen who die at sea; Irish dialect
The Old Lady Shows Her Medals	Barrie	2M	3F	Comedy	Cockney and Scotch charwomen dream of sons in the war
The Lesson	Ionesco	1M	2F	Drama	Satire on education, language, and communication

Title	Playwright	Cast		Type	Comment
The Lord's Will	Green	1M	2F	Tragedy	Comment on faith healing; folk drama
The Happy Journey from Camden to Trenton	Wilder	3M	3F	Drama	Forerunner of *Our Town*
The Long Christmas Dinner	Wilder	6M	6F	Drama	Several generations celebrate the traditional Christmas
Master Pierre Patelin	Unknown	4M	1F	Farce	Morality play, hilarious
The Marriage Proposal	Chekhov	2M	1F	Farce	For advanced actors
Fumed Oak	Coward	1M	3F	Comedy	English; cuts needed
Lord Bryon's Love Letter	Williams	1M	3F	Comedy	New Orleans tourist and a con game
Before Breakfast	O'Neill		1F	Serious	Challenging monologue
The Queens of France	Wilder	1M	3F	Comedy	Another New Orleans con game
The Hungerers	Saroyan	2M	2F	Fantasy	Expressionistic, tender
Sunday Costs Five Pesos	Niggli	1M	4F	Comedy	Folk tale; girls fight over boy
The Monkey's Paw	Jacobs	4M	1F	Drama	Supernatural suspense
The Lottery	Jackson	8M	5F	Drama	The winner dies
Pullman Car Hiawatha	Wilder	9M	4F	Comedy	Cross-section of humanity
Dust of the Road	Goodman	3M	1F	Drama	Christmas allegory
The Devil and Daniel Webster	Benét	20M	6F	Drama	Folk tale; man sells soul to devil

Title	Playwright	Cast		Type	Comment
The Apollo of Bellac	Giraudoux	10M	2F	Comedy	A secret of success
The Man Who Married a Dumb Wife	France	17M	4F	Farce	Most roles small; a classic farce
The Game of Chess	Goodman	4M		Drama	Strategy and suspense
The Valiant	Hall, Middlemess	5M	1F	Drama	Death row suspense
In the Zone	O'Neill	9M		Drama	Dialects important; a traitor in the crew
If Men Played Cards As Women Do	Kaufman	4M		Comedy	Minor cutting for some schools
Bury the Dead	Shaw	20M	8F	Drama	Anti-war; for mature audience
The Still Alarm	Kaufman	5M		Farce	Satire on remaining calm
Junk Yard	Carlino	2M	1F	Drama	Modern morality; love reclaims junk and people
Mr. Flannery's Ocean	Carlino	3M	5F	Comedy	Study of elderly characters; whimsical
Used Car for Sale	Carlino	3M	1F	Comedy	People are funny—and beautiful

Full-Length Plays Recommended for High School

Title	Playwright	Cast		Type	Comment
Kind Lady	Chodorov	6M	8F	Melodrama	British dialects; all excellent roles; one set
Lady Precious Stream	Hsung	22M	9F	Comedy	Stylized; Chinese costumes; can be all girls
Dear Brutus	Barrie	4M	6F	Comedy	Fantasy about second chance
Night Must Fall	Williams	4M	5F	Melodrama	Chiller; one set; good roles; British dialects
Family Portrait	Coffee and Cowan	12M	10F	Drama	Biblical background; fictional; brother-hood
The Importance of Being Earnest	Wilde	5M	4F	Comedy	The classic of witty nonsense
You Can't Take It With You	Hart and Kaufman	9M	7F	Comedy	Individualists in humorous rebellion
Our Town	Wilder	17M	7F	Drama	Beauty, simplicity; great American drama
The Crucible	Miller	10M	10F	Tragedy	Salem Witch Hunts used as parable
The Skin of Our Teeth	Wilder	12M 2 animals	9F	Comedy	Western civilization and man, summarized
The Cradle Song	Sierra	4M	10F	Drama	Touching story of foundling and nuns
Medea	Jeffers	9M	7F	Tragedy	Beautiful poetry; gut tragedy
The Glass Menagerie	Williams	2M	2F	Drama	Family unable to communicate

Title	Playwright	Cast	Type	Comment
The Matchmaker	Wilder	9M 7F	Comedy	Multiple sets; adventure is fun
The Madwoman of Chaillot	Giraudoux	17M 8F	Comedy	Fantastic solution to materialism's evils
Romeo and Juliet	Shakespeare	16M 7F doublg.	Tragedy	Romantic tragedy; universal appeal
What Every Woman Knows	Barrie	5M 4F	Comedy	Behind every man is a woman; Scottish dialect
Liliom	Molnar	17M 5F doublg.	Drama	Bad man can't change for love; part fantasy
The Male Animal	Thurber, Nugent	8M 5F	Comedy	Rah, rah, atmosphere; academic freedom theme
Pygmalion	Shaw	5M 6F	Comedy	Dialect essential; satire on snobbery
Letters to Lucerne	Rotter, Vincent	4M 9F	Drama	Swiss school; World War II, European accents
Ah, Wilderness!	O'Neill	9M 6F	Comedy	Family life, early 1900's; Americana
Beggar on Horseback	Connelly, Kaufman	16M 5F doublg.	Comedy	Fantasy, spectacle, expressionism
Hamlet	Shakespeare	18M 4F doublg.	Tragedy	Difficult roles; fencing; costume
She Stoops to Conquer	Goldsmith	7M 4F	Comedy	Eighteenth Century; easiest of this style
Look Homeward, Angel	Frings	10M 9F	Drama	Challenging; based on Thomas Wolfe

Title	Playwright	Cast		Type	Comment
Rhinoceros	Ionesco	11M	6F	Comedy	Absurdism with clarity and humor
The Miracle Worker	Gibson	7M	7F	Drama	Helen Keller and Annie Sullivan
The Child Buyer	Shyre	11M	4F	Drama	Parents sell bright children for defense
The Grass Harp	Capote	10M	8F	Comedy	Delicate whimsy; southern dialects
An Enemy of the People	Miller	10M	3F	Drama	Duty of citizenship; is majority right?
The Devil's Disciple	Shaw	10M	3F	Comedy	Satiric look at America in Revolution
Harriet	Ryerson, Clements	7M	10F	Drama	Biography of Harriet Beecher Stowe
Raisin in the Sun	Hansberry	7M	3F	Comedy	All Negro cast but one; integration and poverty
The Diary of Anne Frank	Goodrich, Hackett	5M	5F	Drama	Based on diary of Jewish girl under Nazis
Oedipus Rex	Sophocles	25M	5F approx.	Tragedy	Exciting chorus; Greek costumes
Major Barbara	Shaw	9M	7F	Comedy	Satire on "do gooders"; sets are problem
Androcles and the Lion	Shaw	16M	2F	Comedy	Satire on Christian martyrs in Rome
Barefoot in Athens	Anderson	16M	2F	Comedy	To his wife, Socrates was a bum
Inherit the Wind	Lawrence, Lee	23M	7F	Drama	Scopes monkey trial drama
Ladies in Retirement	Percy, Denham	1M	6F	Melodrama	Chiller; good female roles

Title	Playwright	Cast		Type	Comment
A Majority of One	Spigelgass	6M	8F	Comedy	Dialects—Jewish & Japanese; difficult sets
Noah	Obey	5M	4F animals	Drama	Ham causes trouble on the ark; colorful
Outward Bound	Vane	6M	3F	Drama	Fantasy about death; excellent roles; one set
Uncle Harry	Job	9M	6F	Melodrama	Nice uncle is killer; three sets
The World of Sholom Aleichem	Perl	8M	4F	Drama	Jewish folk tales; pathos; three plays
The Winslow Boy	Rattigan	7M	4F	Drama	Father defends son's honor at high cost
Shadow and Substance	Carroll	6M	4F	Drama	Irish dialect; conflict: mystic vs. logic in church
The Inspector General	Gogol	15M	8F	Farce	1830 Russian satire on corrupt officials
Teahouse of the August Moon	Patrick	18M 3 children	8F	Comedy	Difficult sets; good male roles
Stage Door	Ferber, Kaufman	11M	21F	Drama	Trite, but kids still like it
Sunrise at Campobello	Schary	19M	5F	Drama	F.D.R.'s polio fight; roles, sets difficult
The Star Wagon	Anderson	12M	6F	Comedy	Fantasy of time machine
Abe Lincoln in Illinois	Sherwood	25M doublg.	7F	Drama	Difficult male roles; costume

Title	Playwright	Cast	Type	Comment
Berkeley Square	Balderston	7M 8F	Comedy	Fantasy; characters move from present to 1754
As You Like It	Shakespeare	17M 4F doublg.	Comedy	Good women's roles; low and high comedy
The Bad Seed	Anderson	7M 4F	Drama	Suspense; is evil hereditary?
The Admirable Crichton	Barrie	13M 12F	Comedy	Satire on useless upper classes; British
The Barretts of Wimpole Street	Besier	12M 5F	Comedy	Romantic biography of Brownings
Angel Street (Gaslight)	Hamilton	4M 3F	Melodrama	Psychological suspense drama; English
All My Sons	Miller	6M 4F	Drama	Am I my brother's keeper theme
Antigone	Sophocles	20M 3F approx.	Tragedy	Good women's roles; Greek costume
Much Ado About Nothing	Shakespeare	16M 3F	Comedy	Forerunner of comedy of manners
The Magnificent Yankee	Lavery	15M 2F	Comedy	Biography of Justice Holmes
Elizabeth the Queen	Anderson	16M 7F	Drama	Romantic tragedy; costumes
Charley's Aunt	Thomas	6M 4F	Farce	Classic of man dressed as woman gag
The Doctor in Spite of Himself	Molière	6M 3F	Comedy	High comedy; costume; satire on doctors
Mary of Scotland	Anderson	23M 5F doublg.	Drama	Historical drama—Mary vs. Elizabeth I
The Miser	Molière	11M 3F	Comedy	Farce; costume; satire

Title	Playwright	Cast	Type	Comment
Mr. Pim Passes By	Milne	3M 4F	Comedy	A cute, simple show; small cast
The Green Pastures	Connelly	24M 20F doublg.	Comedy	Southern Negro Sunday school lesson; power
Mrs. McThing	Chase	10M 10F	Comedy	Fantasy about good witch
The Imaginary Invalid	Molière	8M 4F	Comedy	Costume; satire on hypochondria
The Highest Tree	Schary	9M 6F	Drama	Moral issue of scientists and weapons
My Heart's in the Highlands	Saroyan	13M 2F	Drama	Beautiful people; difficult male roles
The Hasty Heart	Patrick	8M 1F	Comedy	Several dialects; pride is lonely
He Who Gets Slapped	Andreyev	20M 13F	Tragedy	Circus performers; tragic clown
Saint Joan	Shaw	25M 2F doublg.	Drama	Historical; religious
R. U. R.	Capek	13M 4F	Melodrama	Science fiction; robots take over
The Rivalry	Corwin	2M 1F 3 extras	Drama	Lincoln-Douglas debates
The School for Scandal	Sheridan	13M 4F	Comedy	Satire on gossip; expensive costume and sets
Papa is All	Greene	3M 3F	Comedy	Pennsylvania Dutch; dialects and costumes
The Romancers	Rostand	5M 1F	Comedy	Romantic style of *Cyrano* in small show
The Rivals	Sheridan	8M 4F	Comedy	Costume; satire; colorful
The Lark	Anouilh	15M 5F doublg.	Drama	Joan of Arc story; costume; levels and cycles

Publishers of Plays

SAMUEL FRENCH, INC.
    East: 25 West 45th Street
                 New York, New York 10036
    West: 7623 Sunset Boulevard
                 Hollywood, California 90046
    Canada: 27 Grenville Street
                 Toronto 5, Canada

DRAMATISTS PLAY SERVICE, INC.
    440 Park Avenue South
    New York, New York 10016

The above two publishers can supply copies of almost all the plays recommended in this text. They will send, free of charge, a complete catalogue of the plays they publish to anyone who requests it. The plays not available from these publishers can be found through libraries.

Recommended Reference Materials for the Drama School Teacher

The materials listed here have been selected for their quality and utility as references for the high school teacher-director in the various specialized areas of the theatre. The list is purposefully brief, so that the teacher may receive the maximum value for the investment of both his money and his time. In areas where more than one book is recommended, the list is in preferential order.

Acting

Franklin, Miriam A., *Rehearsal* (4th ed.). Englewood Cliffs, N.J.: Prentice-Hall, Inc., 1963.
  Every aspect of acting technique is covered and supplemented by exercises selected from standard plays.
McGaw, Charles J., *Acting Is Believing*. New York: Holt, Rinehart & Winston, Inc., 1955.
  A beginning acting text based primarily on the Stanislavski method of acting.
Blunt, Jerry, *The Composite Art of Acting*. New York: The Macmillan Company, 1966.
  As the title suggests, this is a detailed, analytical approach to every phase of the actor's art, from voice development to the use of properties. Extensive exercises for the development of each component of acting are included, along with numerous scenes from classic and contemporary plays.
Stanislavski, Constantin, *An Actor Prepares*. New York: Theatre Arts Books, 1936.
  The original source for what has come to be known as "The Method" is presented as dialogue between the director and student actors in a series of acting classes.

Dialects

Blunt, Jerry, *Stage Dialects*. San Francisco: Chandler Publishing Company, 1967. Accompanying tapes produced by Science Research Associates, Inc., Chicago, 1967.
The text, which includes the phonetic alphabet and extensive drills and exercises in each of the eleven most common stage dialects, is accompanied by three reels of tape recordings. Using the tapes and the text, students may learn these dialects in the same manner that has been so helpful to them in learning foreign languages.

Directing

Dolman, John Jr., *The Art of Play Production*. New York: Harper & Row, Publishers, 1946.
This complete text on directing includes the aesthetic principles as well as the techniques of directing and mounting a play. Principles of design and some mechanics of stagecraft are also included. Rules for blocking action, stage positions, focus, and control of attention are particularly useful for inexperienced directors.

Sievers, W. David, *Directing for the Theatre* (2nd ed.). Dubuque, Iowa: Wm. C. Brown Company, 1965.
A highly analytical and profusely illustrated approach to play direction, from selection to the final curtain, with particular emphasis on problems of educational theatre in high school and college. Appendix information on backstage staff and crews is most useful.

Stagecraft

Hake, Herbert V., *Here's How!* (rev. ed.). New York: Samuel French, Inc., 1958.
A simplified, illustrated handbook of all aspects of stagecraft, including design, construction, tools, hardware, painting, lighting, sound, and so on. Especially useful for schools with limited equipment and budget. Can be used as student text even for very poor readers.

Philippi, Herbert, *Stagecraft and Scene Design*. Boston: Houghton Mifflin Company, 1953.
An excellent text in both stagecraft and design, which is well indexed for quick reference.

Lighting

McCandless, Stanley, *A Method of Lighting the Stage* (2nd ed.). New York: Theatre Arts, Inc., 1939.
The definitive text on stage lighting, including instruments, color, and effects.

Make-up

Baird, John F., *Make-Up*. New York: Samuel French, Inc., 1941.
A useful text in the fundamental techniques and materials of theatrical make-up, illustrated with drawings.

Corson, Richard, *Stage Make-Up*. New York: Appleton-Century-Crofts, 1949.
A comprehensive manual of every aspect of make-up for all media, illustrated with photographs and drawings. Color charts and hair style drawings are especially useful.

Costume

Barton, Lucy, *Historic Costume for the Stage*. Boston: Walter H. Baker Company, 1935.
Every aspect of costumes of Western civilization is dealt with in detail in both text and illustrations. Excellent notes on how to construct costumes.

Walkup, Fairfax P., *Dressing the Part*. New York: Appleton-Century-Crofts, 1950.
Costumes for every era from Egypt to the present, with illustrations and related historical data.

Theatre History

Macgowan, Kenneth and William Melnitz, *The Living Stage*. Englewood Cliffs, N.J.: Prentice-Hall, Inc., 1955.
A history of the theatre from primitive to contemporary, with excellent illustrations of theatres and settings.

Hughes, Glenn, *The Story of the Theatre*. New York: Samuel French, Inc., 1941.
A brief history of theatre written so that students find it easy and interesting.

Play Selection

Shank, Theodore J., *A Digest of 500 Plays*. New York: The Crowell Collier and Macmillan, Inc., 1963.
Plot summaries and notes on production requirement of the most famous plays from 2500 years of Western drama.

National Council of Teachers of English, *Guide to Play Selection* (2nd ed.). New York: Appleton-Century-Crofts, 1958.
Listing of recommended plays, giving plot, cast, publisher, and royalty.

Anthologies of Plays

Of the hundreds of play anthologies now available in paperback, the following are listed as examples. A current issue of *Paperbacks In Print,* available at most bookstores, is the best source to locate others.

Watson, E. Bradlee and Benfield Pressey, *Contemporary Drama 9 Plays*. New York: Charles Scribner's Sons, 1931. *The Hairy Ape, Street Scene, Abe Lincoln in Illinois, The Silver Cord, Justice, What Every Woman Knows, The Circle, R. U. R., Cyrano de Bergerac.*

Watson, E. Bradlee and Benfield Pressey, *Contemporary Drama 15 Plays*. New York: Charles Scribner's Sons, 1959. *Hedda Gabler, The Importance of Being Earnest, Uncle Vanya, The Dream Play, Man and Superman, Riders to the Sea, Henry IV, Ah, Wilderness!, Blood Wedding, Murder in the Cathedral, Purple Dust, The Skin of Our Teeth, Come Back Little Sheba, The Crucible, Look Homeward Angel.*

Barrows, *Contemporary American Drama*. New York: The Macmillan Company, 1964. *The Matchmaker, The Caine Mutiny Court-Martial, The Highest Tree, Barefoot In Athens.*